St James' Park

From Shirley Rec to Renovation

1907-2014

Michaela A Lawler-Levene
and the FoSJP History Team

First Published in 2015 by FoSJP
133 Church Street Shirley, Southampton SO15 5LW
www.fosjp.org.uk
email: history@fosjp.org.uk

in partnership with Southampton City Council and the Heritage Lottery Fund

Copyright © 2015 Michaela A Lawler-Levene, the FoSJP History Team and individual contributors

All rights reserved. Except for brief quotations in a review, this book, or any part thereof, may not be reproduced, stored in or introduced into a retrieval system, or transmitted, in any form or by any means, electronically, mechanical, photocopying, recording or otherwise, without the prior written consent of the publisher.

ISBN no. 978-0-9931763-0-2

Layout and design by Anna Vickers, Southampton

Printed by Lulu Press, Raleigh, N.C.

All profits from this publication will go towards future history books and community projects in Shirley, Southampton.

Front Cover image: *Shirley Recreation Ground* - Peter Wardall Collection
Back Cover images: Top (L-R) Mentor Postcard of *Shirley Girls School pre-1912* – Shirley Infant and Junior Schools Archive;
Hicks' Dairy Handcart Shirley – Hazel Crates Collection;
1948-49 Football Team in Shirley Rec – Judy Humby Collection
Bottom (L-R) *1897 OS Map;*
Postcard of *Church Street c.1907* – Peter Wardall Collection;
Postcard of *Shirley Recreation Ground - Pre-Second World War* – Peter Wardall Collection

Contents

Foreword

Introduction: Tania Emery, FoSJP Chair

Chapter 1 **St James' Park, the Former Shirley Recreation Ground - A Potted History by Michaela A Lawler-Levene and the FoSJP History Team**   1

Chapter 2 **A Recreation Ground for the Children of Shirley**

    The Genesis of Shirley Recreation Ground by AGK Leonard   11

    The 1907 Official Opening and 1911 Plans for Shirley Recreation Ground by the FoSJP History Team   14

Chapter 3 **Caring for the Natural Environment**   19

Chapter 4 **The Park during the Second World War**   29

Chapter 5 **A Century of Play - 1910s to the 2010s**   45

Chapter 6 **In Need of a Friend**

    The Establishment of FoSJP by Nichola Caveney   59

    The Lottery Grant Restoration and Renovation by Helen Saward   66

    St James' Park - A Real 'Park for People' Project by Jon Dyer-Slade   70

Chapter 7 **A Long Standing Tradition of Carnivals and Community Events**   71

Chapter 8 **Never Too Old to Learn - Education in the Park**   79

Chapter 9 **Arthur's Bench - A Park Love Story**   87

Endnotes   92

Bibliography   93

Acknowledgements   95

Foreword

It is from discovering Shirley's past from those who have gone before us that we understand the Shirley of today and plan a better tomorrow.

This Shirley Heritage Project publication is the result of a joint initiative between those who have generously shared their photographs and stories, those who have recorded them, those who have researched and produced historical information and those individuals and institutions who made the book a reality. To everyone from FoSJP, in Shirley, Southampton and beyond who have given their time to this project, including friends and family who have supported us, we thank you.

A full list of acknowledgements is given at the back of the book.

We remember those who inspired us, but did not see the finished publication.

Dedicated to the memory of

Monica V Brown
Lynda Chantler
Julie Fisher
Geoff Gravelson
Freda Hancock
Charles Daniel Maher
Jeff Pain
Raymond Quick
Mike Spickett
Doctor J L Struthers
Patricia White

Introduction
Tania Emery FoSJP Chair

St James' Park is a small community green space that has undergone an incredible transformation in a short period of time. Supported by the local community, Southampton City Council, the Heritage Lottery Fund and Big Lottery Fund, the Park has been transformed from a tired green area to a vibrant community space. The physical environment of the Park has been developed to provide updated and exciting play and exercise facilities for children and adults alike. The available green field space has been maintained to provide facilities for dog walkers, team sports and events and the existing natural environment has been enhanced and developed to provide new plant life and to maximise the impact of the existing species.

However, more than just the physical environment, the changes to the Park have enabled a transformation of the local community and enhanced the lives of many of those that live in the local area. The Park now teems with regular and occasional users from across the local communities who come to enjoy its facilities. The café and community room facilities offer regular employment opportunities and provide a welcoming and economical venue for a casual coffee or light lunch and for community and support groups to meet. The development of the Park has sparked a renewed interest in the local space: volunteers now run regular youth, sporting, handicraft, environmental and gardening opportunities in the Park; some run by the Friends of St James' Park and some by associated groups.

Alongside all of these activities the History Team has unearthed local historical information and shared much of this with local people through temporary displays, public talks, educational workshops, guided walks and information displays in the Park. This work has underpinned the development of the Park as a whole and has ensured that the St James' Park of today reflects the St James' Park of the past and remains at the heart of its local community.

We are very proud and excited by all we have achieved as the Friends of St James' Park during our short history. We are proud of the heritage of St James' Park and excited to be part of enabling a vibrant future for the Park and its community.

Tania Emery
Friends of St James' Park (FoSJP) Chair, 2015

1 St James' Park, the Former Shirley Recreation Ground - A Potted History

Michaela A Lawler-Levene and the FoSJP History Team

One of the first written records of what is now St James' Park in Shirley is a reference in the *Domesday Book* of 1085 to the land belonging to the Manor of Shirley. However, this is not the earliest evidence of human existence in this area. Karen Wardley, Head of Collections at Southampton City Council, reveals the earlier history:

"Our knowledge about early human activity in the area which came to be known as Shirley derives from archaeological finds. Gravel digging in the 19th and early 20th centuries, chance finds, and professionally managed archaeological investigations carried out prior to building development from the mid 20th century onwards, have all combined to build up a picture of what has happened here in the past. All this evidence can be found on Southampton's Historic Environment Record (HER) which is a record of archaeological sites, find spots, historic buildings and Scheduled Monuments within the city boundary. This record continues to be updated as new discoveries are made. More information can be found on the national website www.heritagegateway.org.uk.

The archaeological evidence shows continuous use and exploitation of the area from earliest times. The oldest artefacts from Shirley are flint hand axes from the Lower Palaeolithic period (700,000 – 100,000 BC). Dozens of these axes have been found here, and are now held in museum collections all around the UK. These tools were used by early hunter gatherers who moved across the land, following the herds of animals which provided them with meat, hides and bone. The axes vary in size and shape, no doubt for specific purposes connected with butchery or the preparation of hides. The reason these axes are found in such abundance in Shirley is because of the underlying geology. The river gravels here were largely formed by material washing down-river, and include re-deposited material from higher land to the north. Many of these ancient artefacts come from the gravel quarries in the area. Antiquarians, like William Dale, purchased them for their own collections, and later donated or sold them to museums, like Tudor House Museum. In 1898 Dale recorded 18 Palaeolithic axes from a gravel pit "near Shirley church" which may well have been the one on the site of St James' Park." [1]

Shirley Common and Whitehead's Wood

Prior to the Norman Invasion the land was owned by 'Cypping.' However, in the *Domesday Book* of 1085, the Manor of Shirley is documented as belonging to Ralph de Mortimer.[2] The Manor house was essentially a mill, farmstead and pond, but there was also mention of a church. The borders of Ralph de Mortimer's land at that time stretched far beyond the present day borders of Shirley.

Rosaleen Wilkinson, 1997, reveals that the Manor of Shirley was, *"probably situated at the junction of Redbridge Hill, Romsey Road and Winchester Road...by the confluence of the Hollybrook and Tanner's Brook streams."* [3] The significance of these brooks is recognised in the names of local schools: Hollybrook and Tanner's Brook Infant and Junior Schools. This convergence of streams is also what formed a series of ponds, subsequently known as Shirley Ponds. This is the area known as 'Old Shirley'. Adrian Rance, 1986, continues: *"Shirley Mill was powered by a series of three ponds*[4] *which lay between Warren Avenue and Winchester Road...all but one have been drained and grassed over, but as recently as 1963 there was good fishing to be had: the record pike of 29.5 lbs."* [5]

Wilkinson continues to reveal that in 1228 there was a dispute between Nicholas of Shirley, the then Lord of the Manor, and the Burgesses of Southampton over cattle grazing rights. Nicholas claimed that lands east of the present Hill Lane were also part of the Shirley and Hill Manor lands, and hence he had the right to graze his cattle. The Southampton Burgesses disagreed, and Nicholas of Shirley was paid *"10 marks of silver"* to relinquish his rights to the land. This defined not only the grazing rights, but also the borders of the town. Lands east of Hill Lane became for the use of residents of Southampton (now part of Southampton Common that we know today), and lands to the west of Hill Lane were defined as 'Shirley Common' and belonging to the Manor of Shirley. Wilkinson describes the subsequent Lords of the Manor of Shirley in vivid detail: *Shirley: Domesday to D Day* is highly recommended for further reading on this early history.[6]

Neanderthal handaxe found in Shirley.
Hampshire Cultural Trust/Winchester City Council
Ref. WINCM:ARCH 2144.218

It isn't likely that all the Lords of the Manor of Shirley (and Hill) actually lived at the premises; it's more likely that they rented it out to farmers or millers, like Richard Orchard, a miller, who rented the mill from John Whitehead, son of Robert Whitehead, who acquired the mill in 1433. The Whiteheads, a prominent and influential family, were Lords of the Manor from 1433 to 1777. Wilkinson has discovered many references to the owners of the Manor during this period. As a result of the Whiteheads' ownership, Shirley Common also became known as Whiteheads' Wood or Common. On the 1778 Map, the area is listed as Whitheds wood Common. There have been many derivatives of its spelling, but over the years this has been shortened to Whithedwood. Several properties and roads in Shirley have names derived from Whitehead's Wood, namely: Whithedswood House and its generous Park grounds, which was located between Shirley Avenue and St James' Road, cited as built in c.1820; Whitedwood Lodge and Whithedswood Cottage also on the estate; Whithedwoods Farm - demolished after the Red House at 146 Wilton Road was built, which subsequently also changed its name to to Whithedwood; and of course not to forget the current Whithedwood Avenue, off St James' Road. It was during the time of the Whiteheads that the early Parish Church at Shirley, assumed to be situated near the mill and pond, was demolished. Wilkinson informs us that in 1574 Shirley Parish Church was amalgamated with Millbrook Parish. Shirley Church which had fallen into a state of ruin was pulled down in 1609.

The Enclosure of Shirley Common

When the Whitehead line came to an end, the land was inherited by the Thistlethwaytes (Mary Whitehead's husband's family). They eventually sold it to the Atherley and Warriner families. The unfortunate Gifford Warriner Esq. from the Conock Manor Estate, Devizes, Wiltshire, was declared a lunatic in 1821; his lands subsequently managed by trustees who joined forces with the Atherley family in a joint application to Parliament for permission to enclose and build upon Shirley Common.

This section of the 1830 Enclosure Map shows the junction of what is now St James' Road and Winchester Road, where the Park is now. Anglesea Road is already marked out (bottom left corner) as is Bellemoor Road and the short section of what is now Wilton Road (between Bellemoor Road and Winchester Road). It even states on the map that it is owned by 'The Trustees of Gifford Warriner Esq.- a Lunatic'. The enclosure of Shirley Common was granted on 22nd May 1829. John Hayward was the surveyor and J.D. Doswell laid out the boundaries of carriageways, bridleways, footways and fields.

One of the initial landowners who bought prolific amounts of land from the Trustees of Gifford Warriner was Nathaniel Newman Jefferys, a local philanthropist, who built the substantial Hollybrook House for his new bride Catherine. This was situated near the current Hollybrook Infant and Junior Schools.

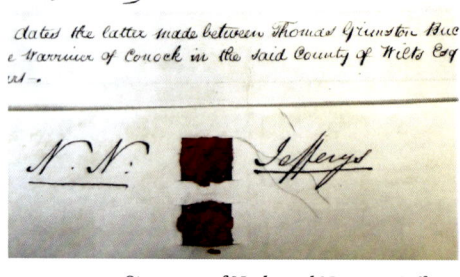

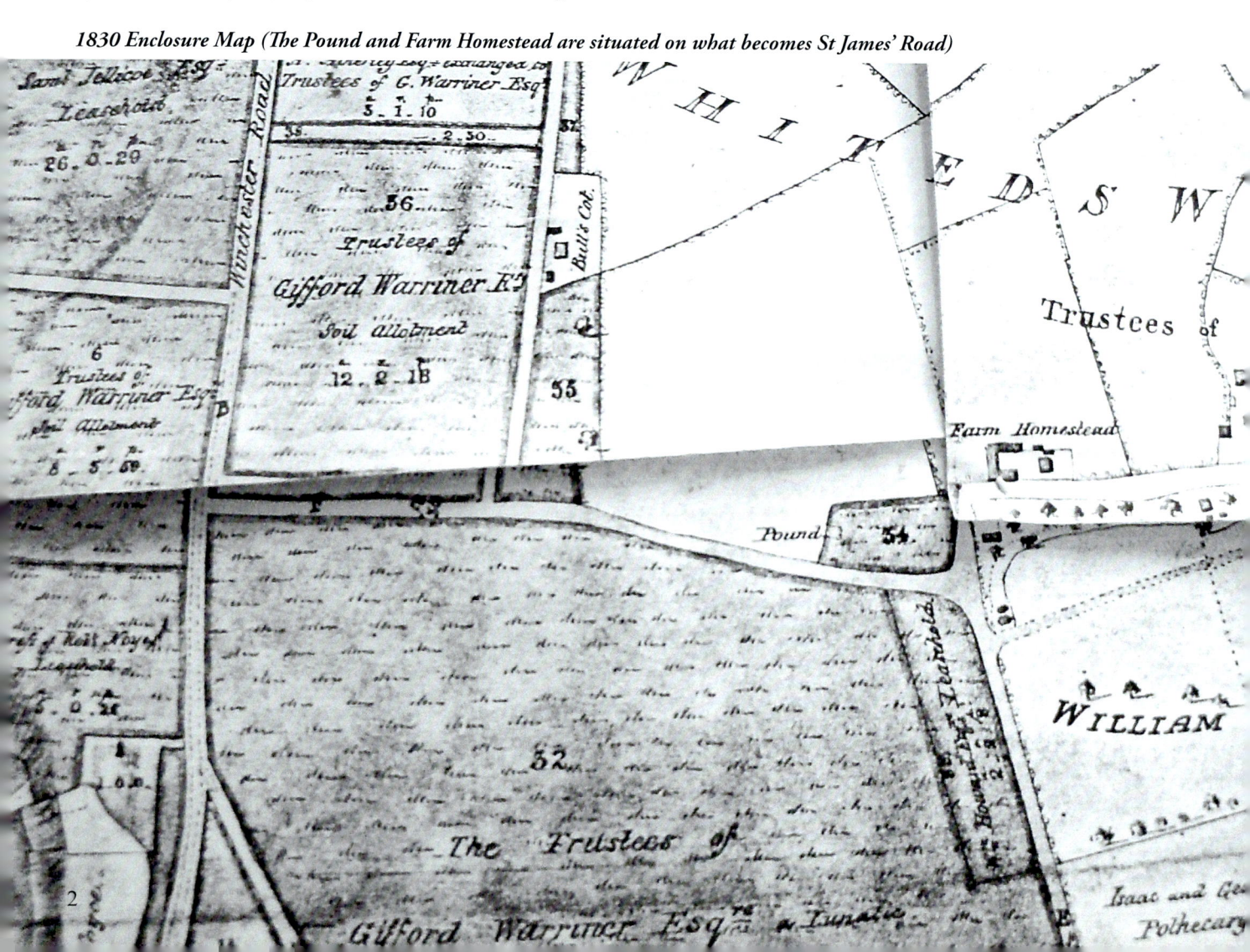

Signature of Nathaniel Newman Jefferies

1830 Enclosure Map (The Pound and Farm Homestead are situated on what becomes St James' Road)

'Coastal Scene' William Shayer. Southampton City Art Gallery HMPS_SCAG_498

'New Shirley' on Shirley Common, soon began to emerge: a fashionable and genteel Shirley, with impressive country houses, villas, lodges and estates. As New Shirley was up the hill from the original village of Shirley, it also became known as 'Upper Shirley'.

"Villas are fast rising there, creating the appearance of a populous and genteel occupation of what is well known to be one of the most beautiful and healthy spots in our picturesque neighbourhood."

At this time Shirley was still a pretty rural village, occupied by people who worked the land: it was considered a genteel area in which to take a country walk, especially towards the Hill Lane area. Parts of Shirley Common were seasonally frequented by travelling people, known then as 'gypsies', and they were often favourite subjects in the paintings of William Shayer, a renowned artist, who eventually moved with his family to 'Bladon Lodge' on Winchester Road (near the junction with Dale Road). Nathaniel Jefferys commissioned Shayer to paint several religious paintings for St James' Church which William Shayer and Nathaniel and Catherine Jefferys attended. The Jefferys are entombed in the catacombs and Shayer is buried in the Church grounds. Shayer Road, near St James' Church, takes its name from this famous resident.

It's difficult to know whether Shayer painted these particular rural paintings in Shirley, as he also enjoyed painting scenes from the New Forest and elsewhere in Hampshire. However, Shirley at the time of Shayer was indeed a country village, with cattle, woodland and rolling hills down to water. They certainly give us an indication of what rural life could have been like during

'A Shady Corner' William Shayer. Southampton City Art Gallery HMPS_SCAG_1341

'Gypsies in the Wood' William Shayer. Southampton City Art Gallery HMPS_SCAG_500

the mid 19th Century. As the fields became divided into generous building plots, both New Shirley and the area around Old Shirley and Shirley Ponds became popular places for professionals, artists, clergymen, entrepreneurs and sea captains to live. One of the most popular spots was 'The Crescent' close to Shirley Ponds, which boasted generous villas with coach houses on exceptionally large plots, many with waterside views.

Shirley Parish Church and Vicarage

As befitting any genteel area, the residents required a church in which to worship. In 1835, Nathaniel Newman Jefferys donated land on which the new Shirley Parish Church (now also known as St James' Church) was erected. This was established mainly with funding from its first vicar, the Reverend William Orger (Vicar 1837-1859). The church was consecrated by the Bishop of Winchester in August 1836.[13] This building, designed by William Hinves, is now Grade II listed and sits within the St James' Road Conservation Area.[14]

The first Vicarage, Oakfield House, also built in the 1830s, was situated on Winchester Road, directly opposite the Park, by the Wordsworth Road/Winchester Road entrance. This building eventually became part of the expanding Children's Hospital, which was next door at Anglesea House. The Children's Hospital closed and moved to the Southampton General site in 1974. The original Vicarage of Shirley Parish was demolished in 2009: flats are now built in its place. On 29th June 1921, Hanover Lodge, Church Street was purchased as the Parsonage House for Bernard Cecil Jackson, Vicar of Shirley. The third and final position for the Vicarage is the current location on Wordsworth Road. All three properties overlooked the Church and the Park.

The majority of the early Shirley Parish Georgian properties are recognisable by their yellow brick, believed to be the local 'Beaulieu Buff' bricks, from the New Forest, Hampshire.[15]

In 1840, Nathaniel Jefferys also owned a large plot of land opposite the Parish Church, then a pasture (now the Park). By the mid 1800s, as Shirley developed, the area now known as St James' Park was surrounded by beautiful Victorian and Georgian villas which were built as early as 1835.[16,17] One can perhaps imagine the idyllic 1840s image of the Church with grazing animals in the field opposite and the beautiful villas around it (some still in existence today). It is an image that perhaps Nathaniel Jefferys wanted to preserve, for in 1851 Mr Jefferys had the foresight to place a restrictive covenant on the land which stated that it could 'be used for arable or pasture, but it could not be built upon.'[18] - a covenant that spared the land from development and ensured the green space so loved today.

If it is difficult to picture an idyllic rural scene in an area where green space is now a rarity, perhaps this Victorian portrayal of 'Old Shirley' will help. It was at first thought to be a William Shayer painting, but Southampton Art Gallery Curator, Tim Craven, has explained that the quality of the painting, especially the trees and leaves, are lacking Shayer's expertise. Tim's predecessor had decided that

The Crescent, Shirley Warren, c.1890 - Freda Hancock Collection [12]

it wasn't of sufficient quality to be regarded as a Shayer piece. However, as Tim pointed out, the sky shows some possibility of Shayer's artistry. This scene is possibly the result of collaboration with another artist, something that Shayer did frequently, especially with his children, several of whom followed in his footsteps to also become artists themselves. Although likely to be 19th Century, as a possible collaboration, it can only be listed as 'British School'.

Having seen the picture of 'Old Shirley' it becomes easier to visualise a landscape where flowers, fruits and vegetables were produced both for local consumption and also for the ships in Southampton Port. Goods were transported by handcart, horse and cart and also on horseback. Shayer who was fascinated with rural life, captures these images in many of his paintings. In keeping with the Jefferys's covenant, in the 1860s the land on which is now the Park became a garden nursery: one of many in this primarily rural area. Upper Shirley and Hill were well known for their flowers and market gardens.

'Old Shirley' British School, Unamed. Southampton City Art Gallery HMPS_SCAG_495

St James' Park a pasture in 1840

The Parish of Millbrook Tithe Map 1840
Hampshire Record Office: 21M65/F7/213/

The Didcot, Newbury and Southampton Railway Line

Building development was not the only threat to agricultural land. In May 1840 the railway line between London and Southampton had become operational. During 1881-1884 Shirley almost had its own railway station. Vast amounts of land were fenced off for the Didcot, Newbury and Southampton line, which was due to link Southampton via Newbury and Didcot to the industrial cities of the Midlands and the North of England. Southampton spent about £100,000 on preparations for the railway line, but in October 1883 the works were postponed. When James Staat Forbes became Chairman of the DN&S Railway in February 1884, his first act was to stop all works in Southampton.[19] The scheme for the Winchester to Southampton extension was discarded, but the road names by the Park still have a link - Newbury Road and Didcot Road are named after the railway line; Stratton Road was known as Station Road up to 1903, some believe with links to the proposed railway, though others believe it to be named after the Police Station that was also situated on this road.

Shirley Local Board of Health

The Shirley Local Board of Health was established on 25th February 1853, partly in response to the 1849 cholera outbreak that affected Southampton. The members of the Board were twelve of Shirley's most respected gentlemen.[20] The Board was the forerunner of local government in Shirley, and was instrumental in negotiating utilities, such as the installation of gas street lighting, water supply and drainage.[21] "In 1881 the district of Freemantle joined the board. By 1894, the Local Government Act created Urban and Rural District Councils to replace the Boards of Health. Elegant new offices for the Shirley and Freemantle Urban District Council were built on Shirley Road, on the corner of Grove Road." [22]

The Amalgamation of Shirley into Southampton

The village of Shirley was outside the then town of Southampton, and did not become part of Southampton until 1895; and not without protest. Philippa Newnham describes the long battle of resistance to the merger, one that took both parties to the House of Lords. Faced with the whole costs of the case, Lord Moreley, Chairman of the Committee of the House of Lords, advised the petitioners (Shirley Urban District Council) to withdraw their petition before it was presented to the House. After an... "historic' conference... in the corridor outside Lord Moreley's office", they agreed to withdraw: but with certain conditions to protect the interests of Shirley citizens.[23] The Council offices, no longer needed, became the Shirley Library and for a short time Shirley Police Station. At the time of writing it is an insurance office.

The Gravel Pit

By the late 1890s the land opposite St James' Church had become a gravel pit. This explains the sunken appearance of the Park, as the land was excavated below street level. This was to become an important gravel pit, as it seems that it was from here that William Dale, the Victorian antiquarian and part-time archaeologist, discovered important Palaeolithic finds.[24] Although gravel was used in the building industries and in the playground of nearby Shirley School, it was primarily used for maintaining the roads, which in those days were unmade. This required vast amounts of gravel and was an undertaking of the Shirley Local Board of Health.

The proprietor of the 1890s gravel pit opposite St James' Church, was a Mr George Harris, of 'Whitedwood' (the former 'Red House'), Wilton Road, Shirley. As you can see on the adjacent map this was originally named New Road. On all official documents he cites himself as a brickworks owner, though the family also purchased Whitedwood Farm on St James' Road near the junction of Bridlington Avenue.

Mr Harris was a very public man, an employer and a figurehead of the community. When he died suddenly, aged 44, his death shook the Shirley community. The local newspaper read:

"His somewhat sudden and unexpected death came as a great shock not only to his family but also to his very many friends and acquaintances, for no-one was more widely known than Mr Harris, and he was held in the greatest respect and esteem...The Vicar (of St James' Church) enlarged on the suddenness of the event, and said they must all put to themselves the question 'Are we ready to go?'."[25]

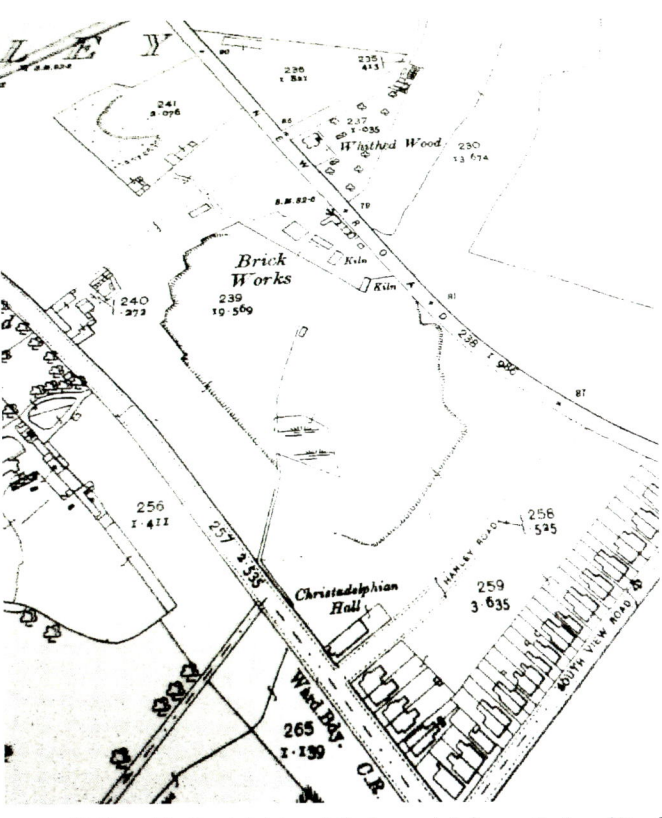

1910 OS Map - The Harris brickworks had expanded closer to St James' Road and Hanley Road, essentially in the area that is now Dawlish and Eastbourne Avenues. (New Road is now Wilton Road)

Pictured: 1) The sixth person standing from the left is Freda's father Ernest William Jurd 1880-1958; 2) The bearded man to the right of Ernest is her grandfather Alfred Jurd 1851-1940; 3) to the right of Alfred is her uncle, her father's brother, also Alfred Jurd (bare foot) 1879–1963; 4) to the left of her father, Ernest William, is Harry Jurd, her great uncle 1861–1939; also, 5) to the left of him is her great uncle (her grandfather's older brother), Charles William Jurd, 1848 – 1928. Freda's great grandparents came from Bursledon (also of brickworks fame) to Coxford, when her grandfather was 3 years old

Brickmaking at Coxford Brickworks, c 1900. Freda Hancock Collection. This photograph shows the presses that would have been used to form the hand-made bricks

Shirley Recreation Ground

After George Harris Senior died in April 1906, the opportunity arose to buy the gravel pit opposite St James' Church. In 1907, Alderman Henry Cawte proposed that the land be purchased by the council "for the children of Shirley" and in March 1907, the council sanctioned an offer of £1,000 to the executors of George Harris for the 6-acre site. In April of the same year a Mr E A Young presented a petition of 1,300 local residents, supporting the idea of a Recreation Ground for Shirley, and in October 1907 the release of monies for the purchase was agreed. Although a formal opening ceremony did take place in November 1907, at which it was reported that every child in Shirley attended, gravel excavation continued for three or four more years. It was then cleared and prepared as a complete recreation ground. It was in 1911 when plans to finally level all the land for public access were proposed.

The Shirley Recreation Ground was in existence during the 1912 Titanic disaster. Despite this terribly sad time for the people of Southampton, there were some positive developments happening for the children of Shirley. The Rec was being laid out and improved, the Shirley School was re-built, the Shirley (later Southampton) Children's Hospital expanded and moved from Church Street to opposite the Rec and the Tudor Museum opened in Southampton.

In the late 1920s, the Rec was one open space with nothing but a football pitch, a couple of benches and a few shrubs and trees. Locals remember it being home to several amateur football teams including the Shirley Working Men's Club. Later the Shirley Wanderers football team played in blue and white and their headquarters were a shed at the nearby end of Stratton Road.

In the 1930s, four tennis courts were built, complete with a hut from where to pay for hiring a tennis court. Flower gardens were established, which were beautifully maintained, and more benches and a children's sandpit were added.

During the Second World War, the Rec was home to a barrage balloon and several structures were erected including a bombproof structure to house the local ARP wardens. This building later became the Park Keeper's mess room, equipment storage and public toilets.

In the 1960s, the children's playground was merely a few pieces of equipment by the side of the Park building but, by the end of the 1980s additional playground equipment had been installed, roughly where the current toddler slides and equipment are located.

With national cuts in public funding, and parks being considered as non-essential services, the beginning of the 1990s saw the last of the full-time Park Keepers based in Shirley Recreation Ground. The upkeep of the Park became the responsibility of the Western Team of the Parks and Open Spaces Department within Southampton City Council.

St James' Park

The Park was always known locally as 'Shirley Rec'. According to Southampton City Council's Parks and Open Spaces Department, it was only renamed 'St James' Park' at the time of the Millennium. By the Millennium, the play equipment had become very tired; plant borders and grass continued to be maintained but, with funding tight, there were no more roses or bright plant borders; and the toilets were closed with the Council only being able to offer essential maintenance. Despite all of those things, with limited green space available, Shirley Rec (now featuring a 'Welcome to St James' Park' sign) remained a popular local park, especially with families, dog walkers, joggers, parents and children after school.

1960s Playground - Joan Cook

Jon Dyer-Slade of SCC opens the FoSJP Kiosk 9th August 2006

The Establishment of FoSJP

In August 2006, with support from Southampton City Council, the volunteers from the newly established Friends of St James' Park (FoSJP) partly converted the building into a kiosk, serving refreshments to visitors to the Park. Famous for its '10p' ice pole, the kiosk was a real success with children and parents alike. The local community supported the work of FoSJP and the membership soon became the largest of its type in Southampton, with an annual membership of over 450 members. The rooms at the rear of the Park building could not be used by the local community, as they did not meet Health and Safety requirements for wheelchair access. To be brought into public use, the building needed updating. Because of its heritage links to ARP Wardens during the Second World War, local historians requested that the Council and FoSJP keep the building, as very few examples of these above-ground ARP shelters remain.

FoSJP ran a series of community events and park maintenance days which brought the whole community together, the largest being the Park100 event on 7th July 2007, which celebrated the centenary of the land being purchased as a recreation ground. Southampton City Council estimated that some 10,000 people passed through the Park in the course of the event. The Park and the FoSJP group soon began to win a number of local and national awards for their work.

The systematic decline in Britain's parks that started in the late 1980s-early 1990s had reached the national agenda and, on 17th June 2007, St James' Park was one of several parks featured in a documentary on the BBC1 Politics Show which highlighted the plight of our green spaces.

Park100 Event 2007

Renovations and Improvements

Inspired by the support from all sectors of the community, the Park and its Friends group applied for and received funding for a programme of restoration and improvements. This was a joint project between FoSJP, Southampton City Council and its primary external funders, the Heritage Lottery Fund and Big Lottery Fund. The local community was consulted by questionnaires asking how people used the Park, what they would like in the Park and whether they would use a community café and a community room. The funding was received in several stages, but the final confirmation for the go ahead of the big project was received on 15th October 2009. Celebrations of the news featured in local newspapers and on radio.

The restorations and improvements were part of a process that was envisaged to take over 10 years: the funding applications, consultations and planning from 2006-2010; implementing building work from 2010-2011; and project monitoring, reporting, and maintaining the new Park from 2011 onwards.

Running parallel to the building project, and supported by the Heritage Lottery Fund, a volunteer team of FoSJP history researchers had been gathering memories and information about the Park and its environs. The initial information gathered was fed back to the designers, who integrated elements of the Park history into amazing new designs. The FoSJP History Team also shared the Park's history in a number of ways - at exhibitions, in heritage newsletters, running workshops for schoolchildren, inter-generational workshops, exhibitions, walks, talks, working with the University of Southampton and Southampton Solent University and via the FoSJP website.

Now, thanks to the Lottery funding, Southampton City Council, the many FoSJP volunteers, researchers, professional historians, archivists and the people who have shared their memories, we are able to bring to you much more of this wonderful story.

It has truly been an honour to be a part of this 'Shirley Heritage' legacy.

Michaela A Lawler-Levene

St James' Park Botanical Walk 2011

2 A Recreation Ground for the Children of Shirley

The Genesis of Shirley Recreation Ground

A.G.K. Leonard
Journal of the Southampton Local History Forum Summer 2007
Originally published in the above journal, reproduced with the permission of the author

The Genesis of Shirley Recreation Ground - now known as St James' Park - is to be found in the minutes of the meeting of the Public Lands and Markets Committee of Southampton Borough Council held on 22nd February 1907, when it considered *"a letter from Alderman Cawte J.P. respecting the provision of a Public Park at Shirley and suggesting a suitable site for the purpose"*.

This was referred to a sub-committee, which Alderman Cawte was invited to attend. It met at the site on 22nd March and reported that *"having inspected the gravel pit near Shirley Church […] (it) resolved upon the motion of Alderman Cawte, seconded by Councillor Lewis, to recommend that a sum of £1,000 be offered for the land, for the purpose of a Recreation Ground."* Its report was endorsed by the full committee, although Councillors Beavis and Line voted against it.

The amount offered was then a considerable sum, worth about a hundred times as much in today's money. The land in question was six acres, shown as 'Nursery' on the 1867 Ordnance Survey map. It was one of the areas from which gravel had been dug out – primarily for purposes of highway maintenance.

The Shirley Local Board of Health, established in 1853, was the highway authority; to keep unmade roads, lanes and paths in passable condition, it required large quantities of gravel on a regular basis for seasonal operations involving digging it out in the summer, then carting and spreading it out in the autumn and winter. Loose gravel surfaces needed frequent attention, particularly to counter the effects of storm water dispersal and deepening wheel ruts.

The highways and other community functions undertaken by the Shirley Local Board of Health in 1853-1895 are surveyed in the booklet *'Shirley Nuisances and Services'* by A.G.K Leonard, published in 2003 by Southampton City Council – available from Central and Shirley Libraries.

Councillors and Aldermen
Henry Cawte (1852-1930) actively identified himself with Shirley through half a century. Born at Twyford, he served his apprenticeship in Winchester, then spent the years 1872-1880 gaining experience on his own account in the United States, before returning to marry and settle in Shirley. There he developed a family business as an enterprising building contractor, whose projects included the Infirmary at Shirley Warren, Western District Schools and the Harbour Board Offices. He joined the Borough Council in 1895, topping the poll as one of Shirley's first councillors following its incorporation into the borough that year. Cllr Cawte became Sheriff in 1904 and Mayor in 1905: the following year he was elected an Alderman, serving until he retired in 1920. A magistrate from 1905, he was also active in various trade and welfare associations and at St James' Church, where he was people's warden for 28 years until retiring in 1923 - to be succeeded by his son Charles.

Henry Cawte was widely respected as a man of business ability and integrity. Politically a dedicated Conservative, he displayed shrewd judgement and independence of mind, always ready to serve the people of Shirley.

To end duplication, Union Road, Freemantle, was renamed as Cawte Road in 1903. Thomas Lewis Way is a recent City Council commemoration of the man who seconded Alderman Cawte's motion in March 1907.

'Tommy' Lewis (1873-1962) was elected for St Mary's ward in 1901 as Southampton's first Labour councillor. He remained a Council member for nearly sixty years, as an Alderman from 1929, and became its Leader in 1945 when his party gained control. He was likewise a long-serving member and later chairman of the Harbour Board, besides serving as a magistrate for many years. He also worked busily as a trade union organiser and as national president of the British Seafarers Union.

Elected at his fifth attempt, he became Southampton's first Labour M.P. in 1929. He lost his seat in 1931 but returned to Parliament in 1945; he retired in 1950, at 76, but remained active in local government until just before his death at the age of 88.

William Beavis, who followed his father as a councillor and alderman, was elected to the Council in 1900; made an alderman in 1911, he served until his death in 1924, aged 65. Himself an enthusiastic swimmer, he was chairman of the Baths Committee for 21 years. In business he was partner, later principal, in the firm of Haddon & Beavis, High Street shipping agents and coal merchants.

He is remembered for the annual 'Beavis Treats' provided for local schoolchildren from 1920 with the income from his £10,000 gift made to the Corporation in thankfulness for the Victory and Peace of 1918.

Purchase

The opposition of councillors like Beavis presaged marked differences of opinion about the desirability of a recreation ground for Shirley and the expenditure involved in providing one.

At the Council meeting on 24th April (1907) Mr E.A.Young presented *"a memorial containing 1,300 signatures from residents and rate payers in Shirley District in favour of the provision of a Recreation Ground."* The Council deferred consideration until its next meeting on 8th May, in conjunction with the notice of motion on the agenda in the name of Alderman Cawte.

It was then resubmitted by the Town Clerk, who also read a letter from the secretary of the Shirley Conservative Association forwarding a resolution approving the proposed purchase of land for a Recreation Ground.

Alderman Cawte formally moved that *"the recommendation of the Public Lands & Markets Committee meeting of 22 March to offer £1,000 for purchase of certain land at Shirley for the purpose of a Recreation Ground be adopted."* This was eventually carried by a vote of 23-13, indicative of some cross-party divisions on the contentious issue.

The report of the Council debate on this issue occupied nearly two close-printed columns in the following Saturday's issue of the *Southampton Times*, the local weekly published at one (old) penny.

Alderman Cawte referred to *"the crowded population at Shirley, where there were now 20,000 people and in a very few years there would be 30,000. There was no piece of ground where the children (nearly 1,000 at three schools) could go to play away from the roads. He remarked on how well off the older parts of the town were in respect of parks and open spaces and reminded the Council that Shirley ratepayers helped to pay for these advantages, although they were too far away to enjoy them ... he hoped the Council would act fairly towards Shirley."*

His seconder, Councillor Weston, *"considered it was true economy to purchase six acres of land for £1,000 and if a recreation ground for Freemantle could be secured on the same conditions he would hold up both hands in favour of it."*

Alderman Gayton hoped that *"the syndicate of gentlemen who owned this land would have had a kindly feeling towards the inhabitants of Shirley and the district, seeing that the land was useless to them for building and they had taken out of it all they could get, by making a present to the Corporation of the land. He argued that the nearness of the Common made a recreation ground unnecessary for Shirley"* – a view later echoed by other speakers.

Cllr Hamilton thought that *"it was not enough to say that a recreation ground would cost £1,000 because a great deal of extra expense would be necessary to make a proper ground. He suggested that recreative accommodation might be provided by a large playground attached to the proposed new schools at Shirley."*

Several other members spoke in favour of the proposed land purchase. Cllr Park recalled that the Council had paid £6,000 for a gravel pit at Bitterne, while Cllr Etheridge *"considered members representing the older parts of the town by opposing the proposal showed they were intensely selfish."* Cllr Pitt elicited the fact that not all the gravel had been extracted from the pit and that if the Council purchased the ground they would be entitled to any gravel remaining there. It was also said that the tenants of the land were obliged by their lease to level it before they gave up possession.

Other members advocated economy in Council expenditure, fearing purchase would involve future maintenance costs that would increase the rates. Cllr Lewis foresaw further development at Shirley and thought they would soon have difficulty in securing open space there if they did not adopt the present proposal. After more members had spoken for and against, a recorded vote was taken in favour. *"The result was received with applause."*

Following this vote, application was duly made to the Local Government Board for sanction to borrow £1,000 for purchase of the land. *"Having considered the matter from a financial standpoint,"* the Council's Finance Committee resolved in June that *"it saw no objection to the proposed expenditure, subject to loan sanction being first obtained."* Two councillors dissented.

Meanwhile, the Council meeting of 22nd May had been informed that the owner was willing to accept the sum of £1,000 offered for the land. His solicitors Messrs Goater & Blatch facilitated progress of the sale by providing a draft contract.

At its next meeting on 28th June the Public Lands and Markets Committee received a report from the Town Clerk saying that he had consulted Counsel about the restrictive covenants contained in an indenture of 1851 limiting use to pasture, arable or garden land, with no building whatsoever to be erected thereon. Notwithstanding these restrictions, he advised that the Corporation could buy the land for its statutory purposes, under the provisions of the Public Health Act 1875 and *'lay out, plant, improve and maintain ... for the purpose of being used as pleasure grounds."*

In October the Committee was duly notified that the Local Government Board had given sanction *"to the borrowing of the sum of £1,000 for the purchase of land situated between St James' Road and Wordsworth Road, Shirley, for the purpose of public walks and pleasure grounds."*

Layout

Purchase having been achieved comparatively speedily, the laying out of the ground proved to be a more prolonged process.

The Distress Committee took an interest in the project and in January 1908 asked that *"in the event of extra labour being required in the digging out of gravel from this ground, application be made to the Labour Bureau for such labour."* The Public Lands and Markets Committee meanwhile *"directed the Borough Engineer to remove such gravel as he may require, the committee to be credited with the value of the material removed, and to employ one of the men engaged on the roads in the District in levelling the land, an allowance to be made to the Distress Committee in respect of the labour of excavating and screening the gravel."* In January the Committee ordered a bar or fence to be placed across the entrance but in June it received a letter from Dr. W.W. McKeith, concerned about *"the condition of this ground for children."* Following the Borough Engineer's report, it was resolved that *"the Committee have taken every precaution for the protection of the children."*

At its meeting on 27th November 1908 the Borough Engineer submitted plans for laying out the ground; these were referred to a sub-committee, which met on 6th January 1909. Next day the full Committee approved its report and the plans, directing the Borough Engineer *"to continue the work of levelling the ground and making up the banks surrounding it [...] also that the footway leading from a site opposite Shirley Church to Stratton Road be closed."* The Borough Engineer was authorised to *"make good the fence around Shirley Recreation Ground at a cost not exceeding £20."*

At its next meeting, on 28th February, the Committee decided that *"the work of levelling be continued as far as possible and the laying out of the ground be deferred until the Autumn."* Before then, the Council again took a direct interest in the matter. At its meeting on 9th June 1909, upon the motion of the Sheriff, Councillor Weston, it resolved *"that the Public Lands and Markets Committee be asked to place 8 park seats in the Recreation Ground at Shirley forthwith."* The Council then went on to adopt a further resolution moved by Councillor Wood, *"that the whole matter of laying out the Recreation Ground at Shirley be referred to the Public Lands and Markets Committee to report again."*

Meanwhile, Cllr Wood had secured the agreement of the Committee to the Southampton Town Band playing there on a Wednesday evening, 8th August, the performance being transferred from the Common. (A request for bandsmen in uniform to travel by 'car' at workmen's rates was unkindly turned down by the Tramways Committee.)

In September, the Shirley Ward Conservative Association sent a letter to the Committee *"expressing the opinion that no path should be allowed across the ground after the land had been properly laid out."*

When the Borough Council met on 24th November Councillors Weston and Wood unsuccessfully moved that the Committee *"be forthwith requested to complete the Shirley Recreation Ground."* Mr Weston said *"there was no rhyme or reason in leaving the place as it was; it was a disgrace to all concerned."* Instead of this, the Council adopted an amendment from Aldermen Hollis and Hutchins that *"the whole matter be referred to the Public Lands and Markets Committee to consider and report upon, Councillor Weston to be added to the committee for the consideration of this special matter."*

Shirley Recreation Ground was becoming a *"special matter"*, the subject of an on-going mini-saga ... It was again considered by the Public Lands and Markets Committee, meeting on the last day of 1909, with the Mayor, Alderman Sharp, taking the chair. The Borough Engineer *"was directed to report on the cost of levelling the ground and the carrying out of other necessary works."*

The Mayor also presided at the Committee's next meeting, on 28th January 1910, when *"the Borough Engineer reported that he estimated the cost of levelling the Recreation Ground at Shirley and the carrying out of certain works in connection therewith in accordance with the plan submitted at £450."*

Councillors Weston and Wood proposed that application be made to the Local Government Board for sanction to borrow the sum of £1,000 *"for carrying out the scheme now submitted by the Borough Engineer and for completing the layout of the Recreation Ground."* Upon a show of hands, this motion was lost and the Committee adopted the Mayor's proposal *"that the sum of £450 be expended [...] in accordance with the scheme submitted by the Borough Engineer."*

This was reported to the February meeting of the Council's Finance Committee, which agreed *"to concur in the expenditure"*, but matters still progressed slowly. Nothing more is recorded until the Council meeting on 27th July 1910, when Councillors Ryder and Wood moved that the Borough Engineer *"be instructed to forthwith carry out the improvements at the Shirley Recreation Ground, as sanctioned by the Council."* To this, the Mayor moved an amendment that application be made to the Local Government Board for sanction to borrow £450 to carry out the works envisaged. This was carried upon a show of hands, the votes not being recorded.

Receipt of loan sanction was reported in November - although in the reduced sum of £389, because the Board had deducted £61, *"which had been added in the event of work being carried out by unemployed labour."* Evidently the Recreation Ground was not to be regarded as a job-creation project ... although it had come to occupy many man-hours of Council, committee and administrative time.

The next step was taken at the Public Lands and Markets Committee meeting on 4th January 1911, when Councillor Kimber – newly elected for the Highfield ward in November – proposed that *"tenders be invited for the laying out of Shirley Recreation Ground."* This was duly carried, after rejection of Cllr Line's amendment that the work should be carried out by direct labour.

(Alderman Sir Sidney Kimber included reference to this meeting in his volume of reminiscences Thirty-eight Years of Public Life in Southampton, 1910-1948, published in 1949).

On 24th February 1911 three tenders were reported to the Committee *"for the whole of the proposed works in levelling, forming terraces and filling in banks in accordance with the plan, specifications and conditions prepared by the Borough Engineer."* It was resolved to accept the lowest, that of F. Osman & Co., at £480 – except for the portion relating to the provision and laying of turfs to terraces and slopes (this presumably to be undertaken by the Council's own labour force).

At the same meeting the Committee resolved to apply for loan sanction of £365, the estimated cost of providing and fixing iron railings and seats. On 30th June it considered nine tenders received for supply and delivery of wrought iron fencing, gates and six garden seats. It accepted the third lowest, that of the local firm of W. Dibben & Sons, in the sum of £170 - £5 less than the lowest from a Workington company.

The Committee also received a letter from the National Telephone Company about removing its pole from the centre of the Recreation Ground and replacing it with two new poles on the north and south sides of the ground. In July, the Chairman and Vice-Chairman met the Company's representative on site and agreed arrangements … including an annual rental charge of 5 shillings for each pole.

There are no further references to the Shirley Recreation Ground in committee and Council minutes over the ensuing 18 months, so it would seem that all the proposed work on the ground had been carried out, without the need for further discussion. As there does not seem to have been any formal opening ceremony, it is likely that local people simply extended their use of the area and enjoyed its newly created amenities as they became available. [Editor's note... see the following section for information since unearthed by the FoSJP History Team, including a formal opening ceremony].

In January 1913 the subject of planting trees in the Recreation Ground was raised by the Public Lands and Markets Committee. A sub-committee met on the site on 23rd January and recommended that *"ornamental trees be planted on each side of the main entrance at end of each flight and beds of variegated shrubs be planted at the NE and SW corners of the Ground."*

It was also agreed that *"trees be planted along the banks encircling the grounds at a distance of 30 yards apart, the selection of the trees to be left to Alderman Oakley and the Superintendant."* Another decision was that *"the gravel path be continued around the ground and that the entrance opposite Didcot Road be removed southward to a site opposite Stratton Road."* Committee business at the meeting on 28th February included a resolution that *"provision of a small iron fence for protection of shrubs at Shirley Recreation Ground be referred to the Chairman (Alderman Sharp) and Alderman Oakley with power to act."*

With these matters settled, little more is recorded about the Recreation Ground, which by then must have become established and appreciated as a community amenity - as evidenced by the only other Committee decision of 1913. This was taken at its June meeting when it granted permission for the Shirley Church Parade on behalf of local charities to take place there on 20th July.

The 1907 Official Opening and the 1911 Plans for Shirley Recreation Ground
FoSJP History Team

As stated by Mr Leonard, no record could be found in Southampton Council minutes of an opening ceremony for Shirley Recreation Ground, so it was assumed that there was not one. Imagine the surprise when, in 2011, the FoSJP History Team was researching in the Hartley Library at the University of Southampton and a rare photograph was uncovered in the Cope Collection (see over for photo). We are indebted to archivists Jenny Ruthven and Karen Robson for discovering this photograph, thus proving that there was indeed a formal opening ceremony for the Shirley Recreation Ground on 2nd November 1907. Several local Councillors are in attendance, including Alderman Cawte who proposed the establishment of the Ground. It has since been possible to uncover original newspaper reports of the actual opening. It was clearly a momentous occasion. The local paper *'The Advocate'* reported that almost every child in Shirley attended the opening.

Since Mr Leonard's article was published in 2007, the FoSJP History Team have also uncovered these February 1911 plans for the laying out of Shirley Recreation Ground, produced by Borough Engineer J.A. Crowther. (According the 1911 Census, 51 year old James Alfred Crowther, from Carlinghow, Yorkshire, lived with his wife Basey Millie Crowther, aged 43, their 17 year old son, Alfred Dudley, cook Mary and housemaid Nellie at 36 Archer's Road.)

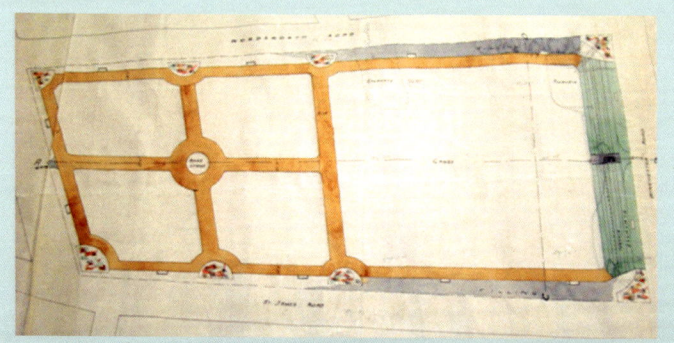

1911 Plans for Shirley Recreation Ground. Southampton City Archives

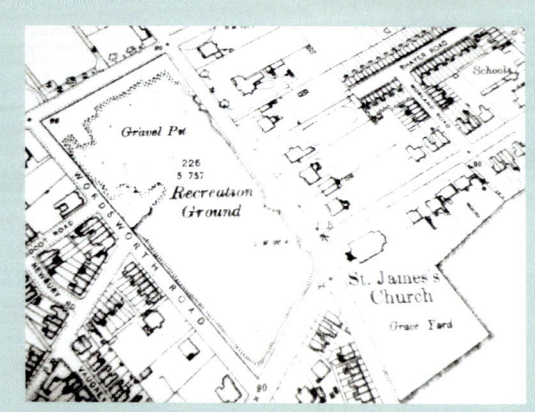

OS Map of 1910 shows part Recreation Ground, part gravel pit. The Council continued to extract gravel until the end of 1910, finally levelling the Ground in 1911

14

'The Advocate'
November 1907
The New Shirley Recreation Ground
Opening Ceremony

We all know the story of the piper who had but to play a tune and the whole children of the district followed him; last Saturday the Mayor and Mayoress invited the school children of Shirley to take part in the opening ceremony of the new Recreation Ground, and, if numbers be anything, met with a most gratifying response, all the children of the neighbourhood seeming to be there.

Alderman and ex-Mayor Cawte, in season – and out some of his brethren in the Council would say – fought for a Recreation Ground for Shirley, and was assisted, to the best of their ability, by the other representatives of the Added Areas, who surmounted, one after another, the difficulties in their way. It was argued that in Southampton proper there were open spaces enough and to spare; thus if the children of Shirley wanted to play, it must be in the roadway, subject to all the dangers of traffic, and we all know what the motor car has been responsible for in this neighbourhood. Eventually the Council was persuaded to purchase some six acres of land opposite Shirley Church, and this was acquired and is in the course of being laid out. The Mayor represents Shirley in the council, and it was thought it would be a graceful compliment were he, with the Mayoress, to formally open the ground for the future use of the families and children in his constituency. A great number of persons assembled on the ground on Saturday including Alderman Cawte, Alderman F.A. Dunsford, most of the members of the council, the Rev. T.W.H. Jacob Vicar of Shirley, Mr W.E.M. Davies (Guardian). Mr J. Lewis and many others.

The ceremony proper took place at two o'clock, when the Mayor unfurled the town flag on the ground, and the Police Band played a selection of music. Then there were sports carried out under a Committee consisting of Councillors A. Wood (Chairman, and to whom Shirley owes much for his efforts in connection with securing the ground), W. Rice, G.T. Othen, and W. Beavis. Some of the racing was very interesting, particularly that for the members of the Southampton Borough Fire Brigade, whilst the race for Shirley fathers and mothers must be specially mentioned. A balloon race attracted particular attention. Many gifts were sent in to render the afternoon in every way enjoyable, and these included presents from the Sheriff, Aldermen Button and Cawte, Councillors Beavis, Etheridge, McDonnell, Oakley, Pitt, Rice, Tebbutt, Weston and Wood together with Mr. J. Lewis. Thus over 1,600 buns, 1,500 apples, nuts, one cwt of sweets, and a thousand toy balloons were distributed, and other presents were sent by Alderman Dunsford, Mr. E. Whittaker, J.P., and Mr. G. Page. To conclude the happy afternoon and evening's amusements there was dancing and a grand display of Fireworks by Messrs. Cox and McPherson.

Since Saturday the following balloons have been accounted for:-- The Mayor's balloon was found at 4 o'clock in the afternoon by Mr. Phippes, Hyde Park, Awbridge near Romsey. The Deputy Mayor's balloon was found at Cadbury Farm, Mottisfont, at 3.30pm The Sheriff's balloon was picked up at 4.30 at Lockerley by W. Betteridge of Green Farm, Lockerly.
Mr. Etheridge's balloon was picked up by Mr Knight's son in the strawberry garden, Dunwood near Romsey at a quarter past four, while Mr. Weston's balloon was found in an apple tree by the gardener to
Mr W Burrough Hill jun., Brunswick Lodge, Shirley.

1. Butcher	9
2. Ald. Bathurst	10
3. — Cawte	11
4. Councillor Miller	12
5. Boro Treas. Anderson	13 Lady engaged to No 14.
6	14 Mayor's Son
7 Councillor Pitt	15 Mrs Wood
8	16 Councillor Wood
8½ Councillor Hirst	17

18 Boro Hill Junior	22 — Tebbutt
19 Councillor Weston	23
20 Alderman Dunsford	24
21 Councillor Othen	25
	26

A Mayoress B C Mayor

The key produced, presumably by the photographer FGO Stuart, is most useful and also somewhat entertaining when you realise that the ladies are distinguished by heads drawn with little hats on them

The Opening of the
Shirley Recreation Ground
2nd November 1907

Photograph Ref: Cope Photograph SOU 79.3. University of Southampton

Of special note is the level of the ground. You will notice that the ground level at the back is much higher and has not yet been excavated for gravel

Edwardian Postcards

In the early part of the 20th Century, postcards were the equivalent of today's texting for Edwardians of all classes, with postage costing just a halfpenny. Subjects varied from Greetings, Comic, Christmas, Art to Local View cards. When the craze took off in the early 1900s, millions were sent, often with a reply arriving on the same day in towns such as Southampton with frequent postal services. Because of the huge number of cards sent, a great number of postcards still survive and are now collectors' items. Luckily these early postcards of Shirley Rec were spotted and purchased by a FoSJP member at a local postcard fair, otherwise they might have been lost from public view forever. Many other local postcard views are now held by FoSJP and cover areas around the Park and Shirley in general.

Peter Wardall

Edwardian postcards from the Peter Wardall Collection

3 Caring for the Natural Environment

The Trees of St James' Park

St James' Park has been described as a gem, a green lung, an urban oasis. This is partly because of the large expanse of green open field that has remained the same since the establishment of Shirley Recreation Ground in 1907, but also because of the beautiful green border of mature trees that surround and protect the Park.

"The most striking feature of St James' Park is the continuous boundary of mature trees extending around the entire Park boundary. The trees sit mainly at the top of banks that roll down into the Park from the surrounding road level. They are mainly broad leaf species, the most common of which are oak, sycamore, lime and London plane. The overall quality of the trees is good, with giant canopies creating a majestic green enclosure around the Park, but a number of trees have been estimated to predate the Park, with a gradual addition of tree planting having taken place during the 20th Century, judging by the mixed age of the tree stock."[1]

The trees by the Church Street entrance are oak and a London plane. Historic maps first show a row of trees on the site, mainly on the Church Street and St James' Road boundaries. A closer look at the map reveals a tree on the Winchester Road boundary and a couple of trees on the Wordsworth Road boundaries. In 1865-68, the site was being used as a nursery (see map).

Not only do we have evidence of these trees on Church Street from the maps, we can see their growth some 30 years later, on Victorian and Edwardian Postcards.

Leaf of the London Plane from St James' Park

1865-68 OS Map

The Parish Church Shirley c.1900 from the Peter Wardall Collection

Pictured standing Tom Hicks (Mrs Crates' father), sitting in truck, Mrs Dorothy Hicks (Mrs Crates' mother), peeping through the float, bottom right, a young Hazel Hicks

This photograph of the Hicks Dairy Carnival float from Mrs Hazel Crates, née Hicks, taken outside the Church Street entrance to the Rec in 1930, also shows the trees. (Reproduced with permission from the Southern Daily Echo.)

St James' Church, viewed from the Church Street entrance to St James' Park, 2nd February 2009 (SCC Park Rangers Simon and Kelvin)

Winchester Road Boundary

As we learnt from Mr Leonard in Chapter Two, the majority of the trees bordering Wordsworth Road are a mere 101 years old!

"In January 1913 the subject of planting trees in the Recreation Ground was raised by the Public Lands and Markets Committee. A sub-committee met on the site on 23 January and recommended that 'ornamental trees be planted on each side of the main entrance at the end of each flight...' It was also agreed that 'trees be planted along the banks encircling the grounds at a distance of 30 yards apart, the selection of the trees to be left to Alderman Oakley and the Superintendant'." By flight, we assume they refer to flights of steps, which were then situated not only by the Stratton Road Entrance but also in the centre of the Winchester Road boundary.

Former Park Keeper, Norman Burnett and FoSJP member, Ray Hancock both remember the southern storms of 1987, which were to have devastating effects on one of these trees. During the night of 15th and 16th October was the worst storm to hit England since the Great Storm of 1703. Ray tells us:

"I have enclosed a photo that I took of a fallen plane tree at the Church Street end of Wordsworth Road. You can still see a slight depression in the top of the bank and just to the right (east) of this is a younger replacement tree...by the following weekend, much of the damage had been partially cleared up."

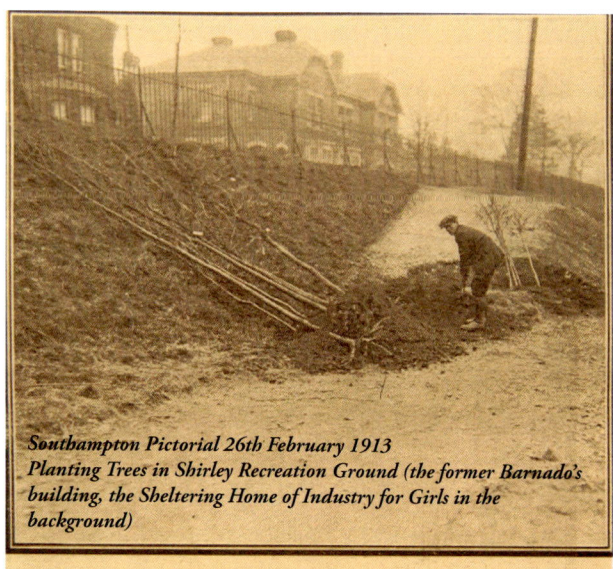

Southampton Pictorial 26th February 1913
Planting Trees in Shirley Recreation Ground (the former Barnado's building, the Sheltering Home of Industry for Girls in the background)

The accompanying photographs show improvements which are being carried out at St. James' Recreation Ground, Shirley. The banks are being planted with trees and shrubs, and the pathways properly laid out.

Photograph taken 2012
Former Barnados building also seen in the rear of the photograph

Oak Tree at the Church Street boundary of St James' Park

Given that the trees by the Church Street entrance pre-date the 1865-68 Map it is estimated that these trees are more than 150 years old.

Trees on St James' Road boundary July 2009

Several of the trees on the St James' Road boundary are Lime Trees. These produce a flower in the Spring.

Lime Tree - also known as Linden

The wood of the lime tree is popular for wood carving.

The flowers are used in a tea, and are known for having relaxation effects.

Norman Burnett, the last Shirley Recreation Ground Park Keeper from 1987 to 1993, recalls:

"I remember the 1987 storms and going to work in the morning - there were leaves and branches all over the road. There was a massive branch off an Oak tree on Winchester Road and it came down the opposite side from Wordsworth Road. I just went up and got a small hand saw and started cutting the ends of the branches back so that people could just drive their cars through. They were the only two main trees that I can remember falling from that storm. After the storm in 1987, the London Plane tree was down across the path - oh, it was weeks and weeks before they cleared it, so you used to have to walk across the rose garden and carry on round again. For people that liked to do their circuits, people running, it messed things up because they couldn't count how many times they'd run round."

"There's another interesting tree at the top corner of Winchester Road. It's one of the trees outside of the Park, it's an oak tree supposed to be a combination of two trees. It used to be very frustrating because in the autumn all the other oak trees would lose their leaves and you'd sweep them all up, pick them all up, get it tidy but this one tree wouldn't lose its leaves until January. I think it was a combination of a Holm Oak and a Cork Oak. That's what I was told. It was amazing, even now it still does this; you can get to January or February before its leaves drop off."

Mrs Wendy Hobbs mentions the same tree:

"The trees on Winchester Road used to be within the Park, but when the road was widened from a two-lane to a three-lane highway [some time in the 1970s we believe], the boundary of the Park had to be moved back. Thanks to a campaign by local residents, the trees were saved from destruction, although they're now outside the Park itself. It seems that there have also been other such campaigns - for example, one to save an evergreen oak tree."

Another Stormy Night

In October 2013, Cindy Phillips from Wordsworth Road wrote: *"A 120 year old tree has yielded to the storm in St James' Park - my front garden."*

The lost tree was another London Plane. Given the diameter of this tree it is possible that this had been one of the original trees visible on the 1865-1868 map.

Photographed in 2013 by Cindy Phillips

Photographed in 2012, trees on the Wordsworth Road boundary

Photographed in 2014, the gap in the tree canopy on the Wordsworth Road boundary. A replacement Rowan Tree is just visible, as is a section of the original trunk by the perimeter path

The Flowering Cherry Trees

Without a doubt the Flowering Cherry trees of St James' Park have been a much loved feature, providing spectacular colour in the Spring and beautiful red and yellow leaves in the Autumn.

During the Park's 2010-2011 renovations and improvements, a tree survey was undertaken. It was disheartening to find out that the cherry trees had been diagnosed with a disease and had to be removed. The diagnosis was *"Ganoderma adspersum, a decay fungus which rots the tree from the inside; the two younger trees are infected with Pseudomonas syringae, a bacterial canker. In each case, there is no remedial action other than removal."* Having just received this beautiful photo (see right) of the much loved cherry trees, taken in 1967, FoSJP conveyed how disappointed the local community would be to lose the trees and it was agreed to replace them with new ones.

Flowering Cherry Trees in Shirley Recreation Ground, 1967. Photographed by Derek Doswell

Photographed in April 2012 Newly planted Flowering Cherry Trees blossoming in St James' Park

A total of 30 new trees were planted in the Park as part of the 2010-2011 renovations and improvements.

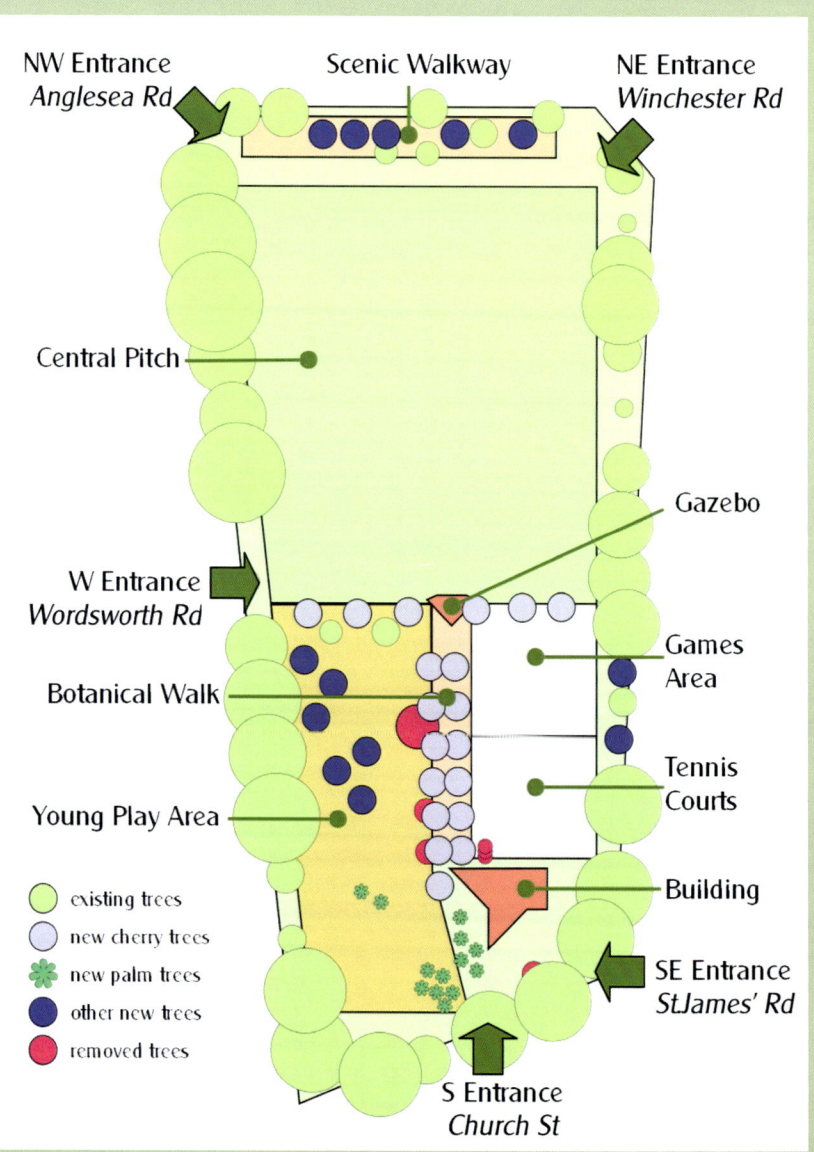

Source: www.fosjp.org.uk

Caring for the Plants and Flower Borders

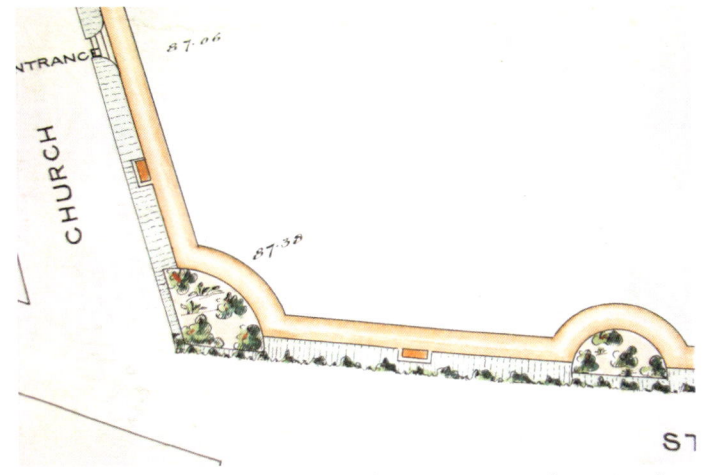

1911 Plans by Borough Engineer J A Crowther. SCC Archives

From this digitally enhanced early 20th Century postcard you can see there has been some planting in the corner in front of the St James' Church area [3]

"In January 1913 beds of variegated shrubs were to be planted at the NE and SW corners of the Ground." [5]

Rita Judd recounts: "I was always accompanied by my mother and never went to the Park on my own when young. In those days there was a Park Keeper who ensured that the Park was kept in good condition. Every evening the gates to the Park were locked at dusk and re-opened in the morning. In the 1930s the inner railed area of the Park contained seating, grass and flower beds. It was purely a formal garden, no playground in the 'Rose Garden' in those days."

Mrs Freda Hancock remembered the fences for the flower beds being installed in 1932. She was 10 years old and living on Didcot Road. Mrs Hancock even recalled the name of the 1930s Park Keeper.

"I can remember it was a Mr Lawrence who lived on the corner of Wordsworth Road and Didcot Road who was the groundsman or keeper of the Recreation Ground."

Don Smith, born in 1926, remembered the flower beds and felt that the black and white postcards did not do the flowerbeds justice. So Don, a keen painter, was commissioned to paint the Rec to show how he remembered it. His painting is entitled, 'Shirley Recreation Ground in 1934'.

Shirley Recreation Ground in 1934. Painted by Don Smith in 2011

Bill Smith, born 1936, comments on how wonderful the flower borders in the Rec looked during the Second World War:

"It was a beautiful Park and it was a big space for us to use.... We had a Park Keeper and he looked after the grounds meticulously in the Park bit - there was a rose garden with beautiful trees, the tennis courts were always cut although it was wartime."

Mrs Wendy Hobbs remembers the Park Keeper in the 1980s:

"In the 1970s and 1980s my son Paul had excessive energy. Rain or shine I used to take him to the Park every evening before he went to bed. I would count him round seven times, to run round the Park. Then I would bring him home to sleep all night! The Park Keeper was permanent then."

Norman Burnett, Park Keeper, 1987-1993, recalls:

"When I first went there, there had been talk about getting the Recreation Ground up in standards, because there hadn't been anybody there as a Park Keeper for quite a while. They wanted this to be a little project and they wanted someone there to look after it properly. For whatever reason, they wanted me to go there and do it. So, I was asked to go and I was quite happy to."

He remembers the planting work he undertook:

"There were a lot of rose beds put in when I worked in the Park, on the side nearest the tennis courts and on the opposite side, Wordsworth Road side. When I was there we put in four big round beds which was all spring and summer bedding. Big, big ones. There were four, they must have been twenty foot diameter round beds which had all spring and summer bedding. I was told that they were hoping that the site for part of the National Rose Collection would go in there, but they didn't do it in the end. They still went ahead and put a lot of roses in there, different types of roses. They used to grow quite a bit of their own plants in those days, up at Red Lodge at the top of Winchester Road. We used to get most of our plants for putting into the Park from there. They used to grow plants for use city-wide. I don't think they do anything now - so there's no nursery work."

"I think some of the planting we did was still there in 2009, but they had put in extra paths. There is also a big raised sleeper bed. We also planted lots and lots of daffodils around the banks, and I mean thousands of daffodils!"

The daffodils that Norman mentioned still come up every year in St James' Park. Even when the Park was dug up for renovations and building work, the daffodils fought through, adding beauty to the rubble.

Ken Prior who worked for the Southampton City Council Parks and Open Spaces Team remembers working at Shirley Rec:

"In the 1980s, I think the Rec used to be not much more than just grass to be honest; a great big grass area and the tennis courts. The herbaceous border was laid out when I was doing NVQ training - we went and replanted it and that would have been about 1990, so it must have been planted up before that. Another part of my job was an NVQ Assessor, internal verifier and we used to have training sessions. Here is a photograph I took of the borders at that time."

Flower borders 1990s

People had really appreciated the formal garden and especially the 'Rose Garden' from the 1930s-70s, and again in the 1990s. When the Park was renovated, FoSJP asked whether a similar formally planted area could be incorporated into the designs, providing the plants could also be easily accessed for maintenance. We were hoping that older people with these memories would be able to enjoy the plants.

The result was the new Botanical Walk.

The children of Shirley Infant School in the late 1980s/ early 1990s enjoy playing on the new park equipment.[4] The roses that Norman planted are in the background

In this 2010 photograph members of FoSJP are sat on the railway sleeper/raised bed before the renovation work began in the Park (there were no roses left by 2010)

Defiant daffodils May 2011 - New stepped entrance by St James' Church under construction

FoSJP Gardening Team, established 2012

After the renovations work was completed in 2011, FoSJP appealed for volunteers to set up a gardening team, the aim of which is…

"To help Southampton City Council to maintain and further develop the planting in St James' Park, in particular with a view to using interesting and colourful plants that will attract wildlife and provide community involvement in the Park."

The Council had always been clear that after the 2011 renovation they could continue litter picking, grass cutting and maintaining a border, as before, but they could not do more tasks than prior to 2011 because of budget cuts. There had been a series of annual public funding cuts since this project began in 2006. FoSJP were very firm that they were not prepared to undertake the work of paid employees, as they did not want to take a person's livelihood away. The Gardening Team met for the first time in the Park on Thursday 12th January 2012, with seven enthusiastic volunteers coming along to meet with Stuart Davies, the Council's Area Coordinator for Open Spaces. The team has also benefitted from a training session from Chris McDonald from the 'Sir Harold Hillier Gardens' (Hilliers Arboretum), who shared much practical advice and expert information about plants. These skills have been shared with local schoolchildren who have visited the Park. Supported by Stuart, the Gardening Team now meet in the Park on the 2nd and 4th Wednesday of each month (weather permitting).

Members of the first FoSJP Gardening Team

"You don't need to be a gardening expert to join us: just to be enthusiastic, keen to learn, and able to commit to a few hours in the Park every now and then."

The New Botanical Walk

2011

2013

The FoSJP Gardening Team get to work

Encouraging Natural Flora and Fauna

The FoSJP Gardening Team has continued to encourage nature. Nigel Fayle, Gardening Team member and creator of the St James' Park 'Bug Hotel' explains:

"The idea for a Bug Hotel (*Latin: Hibernaculum* - honest!) in the Park was instigated at the summer 2014 FoSJP committee meeting. We discussed the Park wildlife area and ways of encouraging insects into it, insect hotels and bug boxes were mentioned and we looked online at various constructions, from simple bundles of hollow stems to large, multi-stacked, wooden pallet creations. We all agreed that the larger ones looked great, works of art with a purpose and function, really cool - if any bugs found them attractive or not, we certainly did!

It so happened that soon after this meeting I had a delivery of paving slabs to my home for a D.I.Y. patio project, and the slabs arrived on two, smaller than standard size, pallets and being someone who can't easily throw anything away (some say hoarder, I say recycler) I considered chopping them up to put in my wood burner and then ping! Bug Hotel! As previously mentioned, having seen photos online of piles of up to five pallets to make the basis of a Bug Hotel and having only two, I needed to be clever and decided that if stood upright, the two pallets leant together would form a triangle, this would give a strong and viable base to work from and also be a more manageable size. Bearing in mind that the finished item was going to be in the Park environment, the hotel had to be of sturdy construction, probably and hopefully, it would arouse the interest of youngsters, who after no doubt putting its durability under test, kicking it and jumping from it, will eventually take a look inside and become curious. To cover and protect the Bug Hotel from the elements, the sides were covered with overlapping pieces of bark-on timber, this was a little tricky to obtain, but from a tip-off, I found a small sawmill at Cadnam who provided exactly the right thing and cheap too, another bonus of living near the New Forest. These pieces of timber were also used to make up the two shelves inside.

'Building a Bug Hotel is a great way for all hoarders... I mean recyclers, to clear a lot of the things that accumulate in a garden.'

Old bamboo canes, broken bricks, corrugated cardboard, plastic bottles, pine cones, broken flower pots, hessian rope, old carpet, bits of unwanted timber etc: all these items were placed, very aesthetically of course, inside the frame and wedged tightly between the shelves. The front and back have been covered with wire netting, not ideal when hopefully attracting larger creatures, but necessary to keep out inquisitive fingers! The whole construction is fixed to the ground with steel rods.

Cut lengths of bamboo were formed into bundles and held together with sections cut from plastic drinks bottles; hopefully these tubes will attract solitary bees, inside they lay a single egg on a bed of pollen, and then seal up the end of the tube with a plug of mud. The rolled up corrugated cardboard is ideal to attract lacewings to lay their eggs in, and all the other nooks and crannies will attract hibernating insects, such as ladybirds.

Out of the over 2,000 species of insects in the UK we hope to attract as many as we can. Butterflies and moths will find a sheltered space inside the hotel for the chrysalis stage in their metamorphosis and various types of spider were the first guests to arrive!

Wood burrowing insects, especially beetles and hopefully the fantastic stag beetle, will find an ideal home under the bark of the Scot's Pine sections that form the roof of the hotel. Did you know that the larva of the stag beetle lives for three to five years in rotting wood, then turns into an adult Stag Beetle that only lives from May until August? Keep an eye out for them in June!

'The Bug Hotel represents an aim of the volunteer Gardening Team in the Park, to maintain an attractive space for all of us to enjoy and at the same time to help maintain the natural environment and encourage bio-diversity where we can.'

It has been placed up on the bank at the Winchester Road end of the Park; this area has been designated as a wild space area and in time we hope to encourage more wild flowers and wildlife into the Park.

So remember St James' Park goers, one man's junk - is another man's Bug Hotel!"

4 The Park during the Second World War

The Second World War had a dramatic effect on the Park and the many children who had used it. Lives would be changed and so would the Park. Members of our community tell this part of the Park's history in their own words.

Memories of Church Street and Shirley Rec during the Second World War

William (Bill) Smith (born 1936)
Interviewed 2010

"I was born in 115 Church Street, which is right opposite the Park. Of course, I was only three years old when the War started and it's quite a memory although I was very young it's stuck in my mind. I can remember the first day that war was declared (on September 3rd) - it was a bright Sunday morning and we were with the family in the garden of 115 Church Street. I can remember a lot of things that happened during the War.

On Church Street - on one side of the road there were Mr & Mrs Curtis: they owned the grocer's shop at the bottom of Church Street - and halfway down on the north side of the street there was a row of shops and there was Halls the Bakers, and I used to be sent down for a loaf of bread and used to get in trouble because, like all children, you used to pick the crust off the loaf on the way back home and, of course, I always had to present Mother with a loaf that was missing a lot of its crust at the far end of it.

Another thing I remember about that area - we had a time when I was, I suppose I must have been five, walking up to Miss Hatcher who was the shop on the corner, to get something for my mother I believe. I heard this noise, turned round and saw coming up Church Street at quite a low level was a plane which was twinkling at me and I realised the 'twinkling' were machine guns! My friend and I dived behind a wall as the plane flew by. This was an uncommon occurrence but not unknown that German planes would come along and machine gun in the street and, at that time, there was no warning - they used to come in close to the ground and of course there was no siren going off.

The war was quite devastating for me - I can remember that during the Blitz the worst time of the bombing, I didn't actually go to bed in my bedroom for several months - I was put into my pyjamas, zipped up in a 'siren suit' that we all had then and put on a makeshift bed in the living room until the sirens went - which they always went - every night - and off we went to spend time in the shelter. The time in the shelter wasn't particularly pleasant - it was cold and it was damp - but nevertheless we survived. We had beds in the shelter of course so with plenty of blankets and things we got quite cosy - at least I was cosy - I suppose the adults weren't... and at that time my father was alive but he wasn't always there because they had to spend time on duty after a day's work going out for what was called 'fire watch', they had to deal with any incendiary bombs that came along.

One of the worst experiences, there was a mobile anti-aircraft gun that was towed around the streets at that time and one of the prime positions I believe was in Salem Street and we were in a shelter not six or eight feet from the gun - you didn't hear it coming - you didn't hear it being towed in position and suddenly it would be fired - several rounds before going off to another position so that the German planes couldn't identify the position - that was quite an horrific experience to suddenly be there - you could hear bombs, you could hear planes but suddenly hear this terrific noise and the shelter would shake when that happened.

My vivid memories are, of course, of our playground which was Shirley Rec as we called it, now St James' Park. It was a beautiful park and it was a big space for us to use - surprisingly there weren't at that time a great number of children in the area. We had our own little group of... I think five of us who used to be always in the Park and it was close enough to be a playground where Mum could come to the corner of the Park, call out and tell us it was time for tea.

'Roll Out the Barrel'
William (Bill) Smith who later became a schoolmaster

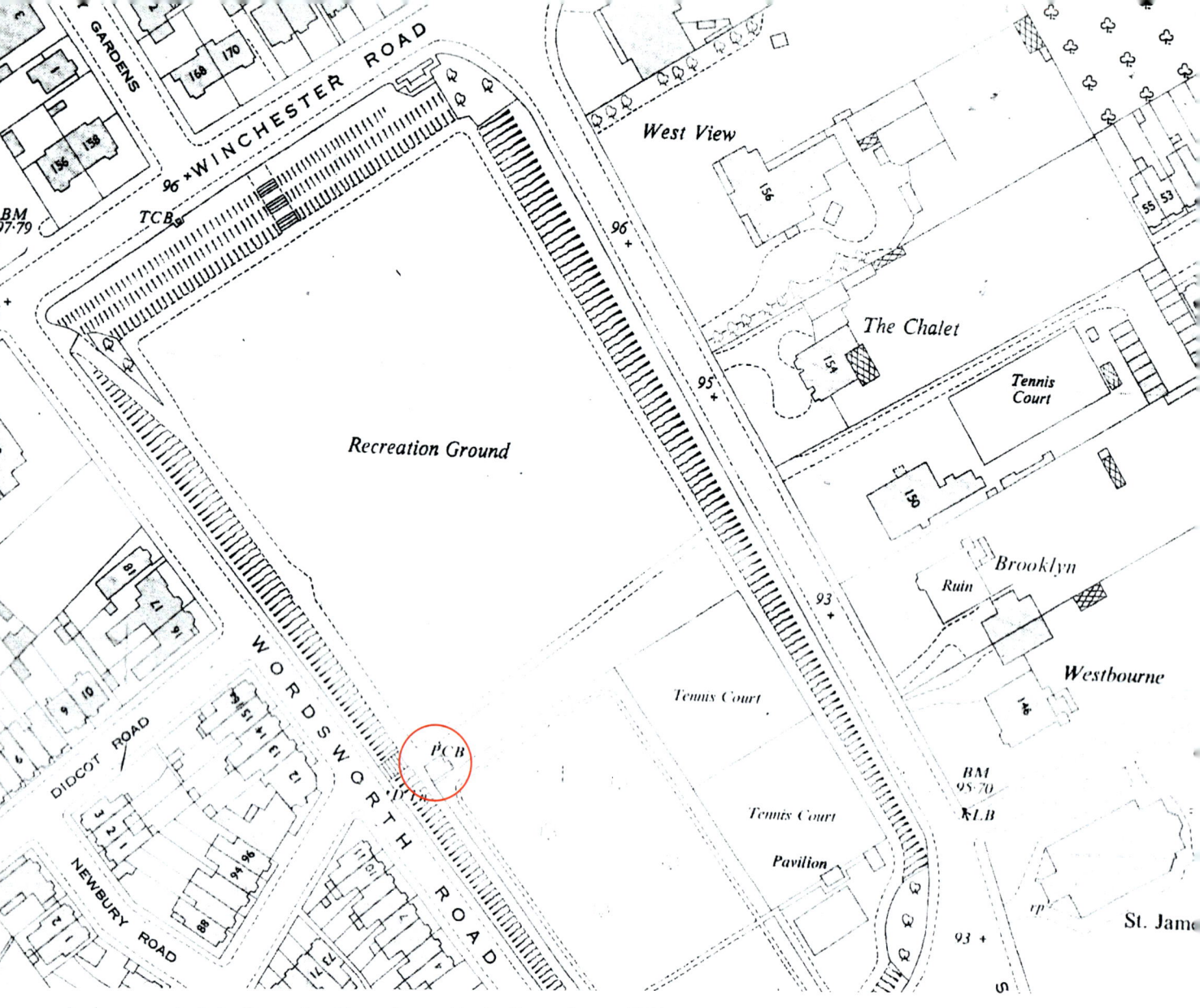

OS Map 1950
Editor's note. The Police Box, situated in the Park by the Stratton Road stepped entrance is marked on this map as PCB

At the top end of the Recreation Ground - outside the Recreation Ground actually there was a really, I would say now, beautiful gentlemen's toilet. Most people would say that it was a horrible old thing - it was taken away after the War, but actually I remember it as a wrought iron loo - it was only a urinal - but it was beautiful iron work with all filigree work on the outside and these days I'm sure it would have been kept for posterity. As I look back on it - I realise that I didn't appreciate it then, but it was a wonderful thing that would have looked something special standing there. Of course there were no loos as such in the Park then so we lads always used to scoot outside the Park to use that particular facility.

We had great fun in that Park - it's not changed too much now [2010] but there were all sorts of things that happened during the War in that Park. We had a Park Keeper and he looked after meticulously the grounds in the Park bit - there was a rose garden with beautiful trees, the tennis courts were always cut although it was wartime. But the things that impinged upon the Park during the War, I think, most of all were the buildings that came along. On the east side of the Park, if you look at it from Church Street, the new building which is still there - we called it the new building because that was the last of three buildings that were built there, it came towards the end of the War as I remember.

Further up the Park on the east side as you look at it from Church Street, there was a building that was built during the war for RAF personnel who manned a barrage balloon in the Park - more of the barrage balloon later.

On the west side close to the Stratton Road entrance there was another brick built building and that was a Police Box and I can remember that because it had a Police telephone in the side.

The RAF manned a barrage balloon in Shirley Rec that went up and down - especially when German planes were about, but one day the barrage balloon got loose and flew off towards Shirley Church - St James' Church - and a dreadful occurrence really because the wire hawser wrapped itself around the church tower and everyone including the Vicar was most upset. It took a great deal of work by the RAF personnel to dislodge the balloon from the church and I think I can remember on the side of the tower closest to what was then the graveyard, now an open space, the buttress was damaged at the side because the hawser broke it away.

Also in that Park in the centre of what is the huge space was a reservoir and that was built after some houses on the St James' Road side, facing the Park, caught fire due to an incendiary bomb attack and, unfortunately, burnt to the ground purely because there was a lack of water. The Fire Brigade had used a hydrant which is outside and is still outside 115 Church Street - they connected their hoses but unfortunately the hydrant broke and the resulting lack of water caused the houses to burn because there was no water available. Afterwards for two days, I think it was, we had something like a fifteen foot high jet of water outside our house. It wasn't summer so we didn't enjoy diving in and out of it - it was just a nuisance - there was water everywhere.

Of course being children, we didn't always appreciate the enormity of the bombing and so on and so forth but we used to go on hunts in the morning for shrapnel, for bits of bombs, and all the lads in the area had huge collections of bits of shrapnel and so on and the bonus was if you got a nose cone from anything, well that really was a bonus. One of our searches... in the morning, took us to Colebrook Avenue which is on the side of the, then churchyard, and to our horror we saw a human head in the tree - there was a huge bomb at the end of Colebrook Avenue and huge devastation and unfortunately this was an experience that I will always remember as will other boys who were there with me. We ran and told an ARP man and we were quickly ushered away from the scene and it was dealt with I suppose.

And of course it was part of Shirley that suffered quite a lot from bombing - I mentioned the bombs in Colebrook Avenue - apart from a great number of incendiary bombs that were dealt with, I believe by the ARP in the main, there was a huge landmine - and we called it a landmine - it was a huge bomb that was dropped by Germans using a parachute, it came down on a parachute, and that landed at the end of Canon Street. I believe the houses between Howards Grove and Canon Street took the brunt of the explosion but it was a terrific explosion which devastated many, many houses - and the blast went for many, many yards. In fact our own house was damaged, the windows were all blown out in Church Street as were others and I can remember two things: I remember that the parachute, a green parachute, that the bomb had come down on, although it was torn, was... 'rescued' shall we say in inverted commas, by the ladies of the area who used it for certain pieces of clothing afterwards because silk, I understand, is very nice close to the skin, so you can only imagine what that silk was used for.

The other thing that I can remember about that occasion was, as I said, the windows were blown out, ceilings came down in our house and those ceilings weren't, of course, replaced until after the end of the War under the bomb damage scheme but I can remember my father who was alive then still - he had to climb the houses opposite 115 Church Street, over at the corner of Wordsworth Road, to get Mother's curtains down from the trees opposite because the curtains had been blown out as well and of course everything was on rations so you couldn't just go and buy a new pair of curtains - you had to have points for that and the curtains were valuable so Dad had to climb the trees and get them down. The other thing that I can remember was that he was washing our ration of bacon in the morning because the ceiling in the larder had come down and the bacon was covered in dust - but it was washed off under the tap and I can remember that it tasted just as good as it was before it had been bombed.

A couple of things that I can remember, going back to the RAF being on the Recreation Ground, there was a building there which I have mentioned but we climbed on top of that. I can remember after the War, it was there for quite a while - at the end of the tennis courts and, as I say, I think that was probably the shelter for the RAF personnel. They lived in tents while they were there. They weren't there for the whole length of the War, in fact I think only a fairly short while, but nevertheless they were there and of course the barrage balloon was wound up and down by a vehicle which was parked in the centre of the main space at the end of the football pitch I suppose you'd call it - it was wound up and down by a lorry that used its engine to raise and lower the thing and of course it had to come down and I can remember also those long cylinders of gas were close by. The RAF men had to fill this barrage balloon up with gas on fairly regular occasions to ensure that it was completely inflated. We used to sit on the banks of the Recreation Ground and watch them doing this they were quite light-hearted about it - but of course we couldn't get close to it because there was a fence - a sort of temporary fence around the area that they used.

The two buildings - the one immediately at the end of the tennis courts and the other at the end of the rose garden - close to the Stratton Road entrance, were the first buildings there and the other building, the main building that exists now, was built at a later date - I can't quite remember when - but I remember the one at Stratton Road quite well because, after the end of the War, our neighbour, Mrs Coombes, who lived in 113, unfortunately had a fire in the roof of her house. My friend and I, we ran along Wordsworth Road and actually went to the Police Box there which had an emergency telephone inside. I must have been about nine at the time - and we called the ambulance and the Fire Brigade.

The Fire Brigade came - it wasn't a terribly big fire but quite devastating for Mrs Coombes but a little light-hearted story, we, being naughty boys - the fire engine was parked in Salem Street and the old fire engine had a beautiful big bell at the front that used to be rung by hand and after the fire was over and the firemen were having a welcome cup of tea, my friend Terry Lochlan and I tied a long piece of string to the bell of the fire engine and crept up the cut that was at the back of our house that led along the backs of the gardens. We rang the bell and then had to run like blazes and I think we actually climbed up on top of the wall of the Vicarage so the firemen couldn't get us. We were chased for quite a long time.

The other thing I can remember - with the build up of the... Americans and our own Army who were on Southampton Common in tents and huts, there was always a shortage of beer and at one time a great shortage of glasses and I can remember one of the main source of glasses were jam jars

31

taken from St James' Churchyard and I can remember seeing soldiers climbing over the wall of the churchyard and relieving graves of jam jars so that they could go and get some beer at the local pubs. The closest pub to the Recreation Ground was the Gardeners Arms at the end of Salem Street.

There was a great deal of activity in the area especially towards the end of the War and there were huge amounts of armour and soldiers in the area and I remember D Day, when it eventually came with huge numbers of Americans passing through St James' Road and High Street in Shirley and throwing money and sweets to the children as they went.

We had fun in that Recreation Ground... sledging on the slopes, I can remember in 1947 we had a lot of snow then and we spent most of our time in the Recreation Ground. We were sliding down those bumps at the far end, which are a sort of series of bumps that, of course, young children enjoyed. The rest of the time, we played a lot of cricket, a lot of football in the Recreation Ground; it was a super space for us and I remember it very well and with affection. I hope it goes well in the future there."

Bill Smith

Shirley Rec Barrage Balloon Breaks Loose

Don Smith (born 1926)
Interviewed 2011

"I have many memories of Shirley Rec because I lived in Shirley High Street and used to play in the Rec quite a lot. I remember they put a barrage balloon in there with the WAAFS (that's the lady operators). There were some brick buildings and as far as I can remember the barrage balloon was approximately in the middle of what was or what became the football pitches - although as I remember it as a boy in the 1930s, there wasn't 'actual' football pitches in there. It was roughly in the middle of the big field area towards the Winchester Road end. You might say along the back of where the tennis courts were and the little ornamental gardens with the fence all round. Sort of running across the Park, from St James' Road side to Wordsworth Road side, they put some brick built buildings in and I think largely it was to do with the WAAFs operating the balloon site and air raid shelters. I would say the majority of the crew for most of the barrage balloons were girls - WAAFS. Invariably there were at least one or two blokes, aircraftsmen or corporals or sergeants in the RAF, but the majority of the barrage balloon's crew would be girls … and there were a lot around Southampton. I suppose it's difficult to put a number on it exactly but I suppose, on a day when there were raids that were likely to be taking place, you could probably count as many as 50 or 60 in the sky around Southampton. Of course they were quite big things - something like about 60 foot long and about 20 or 30 foot in diameter; and I can remember again on one occasion during the Battle of Britain, I was in St James' Road and a daylight raid was taking place - and looking right down towards the town end of St James' Road as you look down there was a row of barrage balloons. You could see many barrage balloons but for some reason or other, there was one section of barrage balloons, there were seven that were nicely in a row, and I think they were somewhere down over towards the Docks area - over that way somewhere - and suddenly a Messerschmitt came screaming over the top quite low - over St James' Road, following the line of St James' Road towards the Common area, being hotly pursued by a Spitfire and I watched him - and he (the Messerschmitt) went right the way down, banked round to the right and went right across that line of seven balloons and as he went to each balloon he shot it down and out of the seven he only missed one and as he went past the balloons, with the Spitfire behind him, each balloon went up in a huge sheet of flame and they actually literally flew through the flames and as they got to the end of the row of balloons the Spitfire shot the Messerschmitt down and he disappeared over towards Southampton Water. In Southampton Water I am sure there are many unexploded bombs and bits of aircraft and so on. In fact it used to be... not unusual for the years just after the War - 10, 15, 20 years after the War, quite often the dredgers in the Docks would bring up bombs in the buckets. That was the sort of thing you would see.

The balloon was obviously sent up quite a lot of times when they thought there were dangers of raids. I believe it was from the Rec that, on one occasion, during high winds, the balloon broke away from its moorings (I'm pretty sure it was the one in Shirley Rec). It finished up bouncing all across the top of the houses down in Janson Road and pulled off a lot of the chimneys and so on with the cables that dragged from the balloon. The cables were on the balloon obviously as a deterrent to enemy aircraft but those cables managed to pull down a lot of chimneys as it went down Janson Road."

Trench Shelter in Shirley Recreation Ground

Miss Joan Greenings (born 1926)
Interviewed 2013

"Denehurst School was situated on St James' Road, around the corner from the Shirley Recreation Ground (now St James' Park) and directly opposite where the Shirley Parish Hall is now. It was a small, single storey building and I seem to remember the playground being at the back. The school was run by the Misses Everard. The Misses Everard lived in the house to the left of the school. I used to walk to school through the Rec and during the War I remember the barrage balloon. I also remember them digging a big trench shelter in there."

REFERENCE

BOMB CRATERS
UNEXPLODED BOMBS

UNEXPLODED BOMBS SINCE EXPLODED REMOVED

FIGURE IN CIRCLE DENOTES NUMBER OF AIR ATTACK IN WHICH BOMB WAS RELEASED

WW2 FACT FILE
SOUTHAMPTON BLITZ

57 RAIDS
1,605 AIR RAID ALARMS
475 TONS OF HIGH EXPLOSIVE BOMBS
2,361 BOMBS
31,000 INCENDIARIES
631 DEAD,
898 SERIOUSLY INJURED,
979 SLIGHTLY INJURED
963 HOMES DESTROYED,
2,653 DEMOLISHED,
8,927 SERIOUSLY DAMAGED,
32,019 SLIGHTLY DAMAGED

OS Bombing Map no.9
Southampton City Council

A Building with a History

The St James' Park Building. Photographed by M A Lawler-Levene June 2007

During the Second World War, St James' Park or the Shirley Rec (as it was known) was home to a barrage balloon, a police box and this bombproof structure, which was built to house the local ARP (Air Raid Precautions) wardens. According to Council minutes *"Tenders for the erection of Warden Posts were considered at the meeting of the Air Raid Precautions Committee on 4th September 1939"*.[3] The building was fitted with electricity in 1942. Notice on the building the lack of windows and sliding black shutters, in case of bombs. This building later became the Park Keepers' Mess Room and public toilets, which eventually closed in the 1990s. In 2006, the building was revived by FoSJP and part converted into a refreshments Kiosk for the Park. A toilet was also re-instated. In 2010-11, with grant funding the former ARP Warden Post Shelter was converted into a Café and Community Room.

According to Rosaleen Wilkinson, quoting Mr Norman Walton, "Wardens were trained in First Aid, identifying gas, rescue work, fire fighting and dealing with incendiary bombs."[4]

ARP Posts in the Shirley Area during the Second World War

Joanne Smith Southampton City Archives, explains:

"The ARP hierarchy in Southampton (ref. SC/CD 2/26) were divided into Divisions. Western Division HQ was at 360 Shirley Road and the Division Warden was Captain GHR Reid. The division was then divided into 4 wards, including Shirley. The head warden for Shirley was Mr AJ Rowland. There were 10 separate posts in Shirley: Post 7 was based at Cannon Street and headed by Mr NE Ross. Unfortunately we don't have a comprehensive list of individual wardens here."

'ARP Post 6 was based at Shirley Recreation Ground'

"I remember being on duty in 'Report and Control' during the War 'Second World War' every 8th night at Shirley Recreation Ground."

Gwendolyn Wardley, 2009

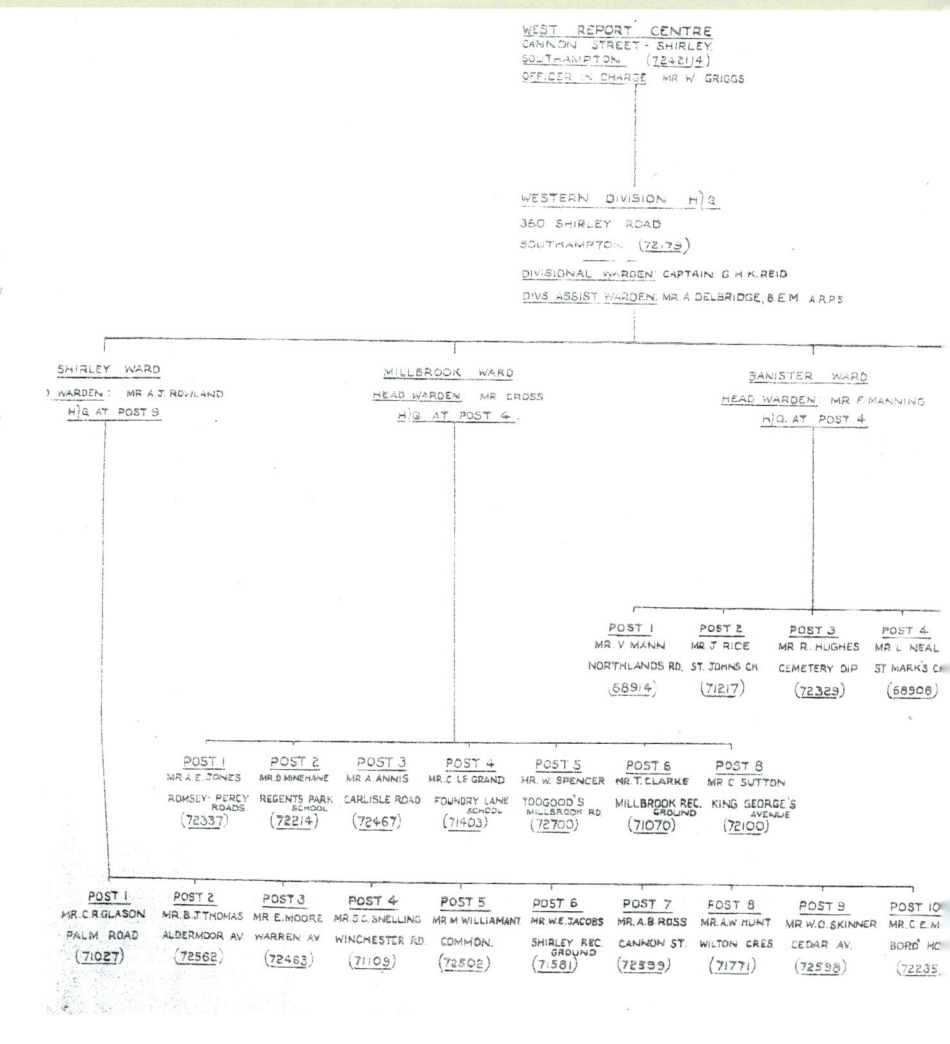

"So, the man in the centre of the Unit 7 photo, without a uniform, may possibly be Mr NE Ross, or possibly Mr AJ Rowland. [Editor's note – he has been listed as Mr Rowland in the Shirley to D Day publication]. The man standing on the left, looking at the photo, of Mr Ross/Rowland, looks like a younger version of my dad, Ronald Wren, but I'm currently trying to find out some more info from the Archives on that, I'm not sure"
Judy Humby, 2014

"I remember Unit 7 - My dad, Alfred Thomas Edwin Clarke, known as 'Ted', row behind girls, fourth from right, wearing tin helmet. There is a further row behind, also with four wardens"
Jo Ormond (née Clarke), 2009

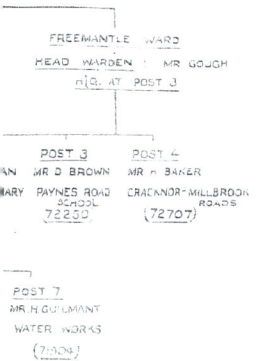

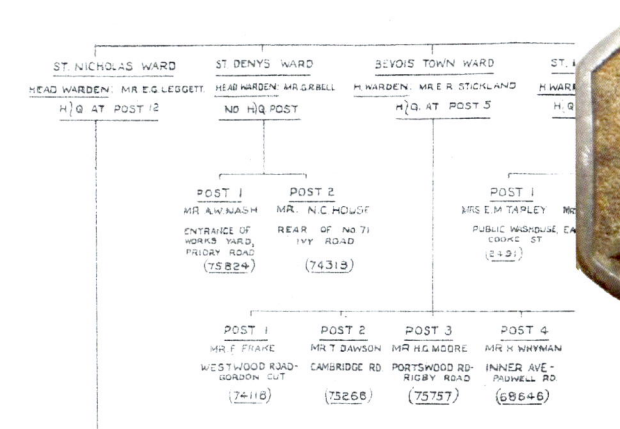

Pictured outside a similar building are: Shirley ARP Post 7, 1942, Southampton City Council, Local Heritage Collections.

(Currently no photograph of Post 6 based at Shirley Recreation Ground is available)

"I was also on duty once a week in the Rec. I don't remember any bombs falling when I was on duty, but I do remember my friend being bombed out of her house on St James' Road when I wasn't on duty."

Mrs Audrey Behan, 2010

35

Mick Masters writes: "With reference to Shirley Rec, I am Shirley born and bred, I was born and raised in Vaudrey Street and am now 70 years old. I have just picked up on your website and I find it very interesting. I note you mention the Kiosk (ARP block). This was used as ladies and gents toilets, the changing rooms for the football teams playing matches on the Park and the Park Keeper used it as his office and store room. My dad, Tom Masters born 1887 (World War One veteran) was an ARP Warden in the Second World War. Sorry, I do not have any pictures of him in warden uniform (just in his football team). The only equipment I can recall him having is his tin helmet and his whistle. I asked him once 'What did you do in the war Dad?' He took me to the ARP control room on the Rec where he reported for his watch, now that building was on the Wordsworth Road side of the Rec half way along, at the bottom of the steps leading down into the Park. If you look at the photo on the history pages on the FoSJP website showing the Park you are right there is no Kiosk (ARP block) this was built a lot later... The control room at the bottom of the steps was also used after the war by the police; they used the phone in a locked cupboard on the outside of the building to report back to Shirley Police Station while they were on patrol. I hope this is useful for the history of the Rec."

Pre-War postcard of Shirley Recreation Ground. Peter Wardall collection

ARP Duties at Carlisle Road, Shirley

Ken Conway (born 1922)
Interviewed 2010

Ken describes his duties, the same duties that the Wardens in the Park would have had.

Ken playing a 'Town Crier' in a Wayfarers Production

"There was a phone in our report post. It was a bit cramped in there because we had about three people on duty. They didn't all stop in there at night as they all went out on duty walking round the roads. We never knew when there was to be a raid, you see. Sometimes it was quite quiet for a long time but then suddenly you got a raid one night, you know, and then everybody was out on the roads there, looking around. I had to report any incidents and they would get the police and the fire service if there was anything there and then they would rescue people. If someone was buried it would be the ambulance. They had to dig out but we didn't.

I was based at Carlisle Road in Shirley and there weren't many bombs dropped. During my walking round from Carlisle Road where the ARP post was, we had a bread basket bomb dropped from a plane. It is a container of about a hundred fluorescent bombs. They all landed in little houses in Carlisle Road. We used to throw them through the window and through the roof and onto the ground and another warden used to cover them over with sand. We didn't get injured or anything, we were a bit lucky.

Another time was when I was on patrol near Waterhouse Lane, I heard a plane coming along in the distance. On the end of Waterhouse Lane on Foundry Lane there was a fire engine so I thought, 'Oh, I better sit down next to this fire engine in case he drops any [bombs]!' and he did! He dropped three bombs on three houses in Waterhouse Lane, (which was just about forty yards away from me). I was waiting for the fourth one to come down but it didn't come down! That was a bit o' luck! It knocked those three houses down at the top of Waterhouse Lane. There was one in English Road but it was done at night and we weren't out at that time, you see.

[When an incident happened]... it was recorded through the ARP control to the top, higher up. They phoned it through to the chap that was in charge of the whole of Southampton. The chap in charge was the Senior ARP warden. The main ones I think had white helmets. Mine was black, with the white letters 'ARP' on it. So that they can see you, in the blackout! They can see the white letters!"

'Oh, my goodness! And did you have to go round saying 'put that light out?'

"Yes! We'd keep an eye on it, yeah but they were very good actually, they kept to it very well."

Ken Conway

OS Bombing Map no.17
Southampton City Council

Doreen's father front row on right hand side, her mother second lady on the front row (on the right)

ARP Duties in Shirley Warren

Doreen Couper née Billows (born 1924) Interviewed January 2012

"I became an Air Raid Warden because my father was a Senior Inspector. There was a brick building built on the square in Warren Avenue and that was the shelter for the wardens to attend to what they were going to do. My father directed them to either to patrol the roads, look after air raid shelters or blackouts.

I would go to work in the morning. It would be dark, no lights on at all and even if you had to have a bicycle lamp on your bicycle that was shielded by a shield. You must go in the morning in the dark and leave at 8 o'clock at night in the dark from work, then go on duty as an Air Raid Warden, patrol the streets or knock on doors for people showing lights. Then when they dropped bombs we had to see and report the different things that happened. When they put the incendiary bombs down you had to put them out with sand and a bucket.

From there, I went to look after the shelters one night and I can remember the time a bomb hit Shirley Warren School, right on the edge of the school. It hit the shelter full-on, a small shelter. My father had a controversial talk with the Philpotts on the other side, where the shelter was, to stop them from going into that shelter. He wanted them to come up to the shelter that I was in charge of, the top of the school, big long shelters, because he could not spare another warden for both shelters. So therefore their luck was in because he wouldn't allow them to use that shelter. So when the bomb fell they were up in the shelter that I was in. The original shelter got destroyed completely; they would be dead and whoever was going over with them. So in other words my father saved their lives by doing what he did.

When the bombs fell and the ground lifts with you in the shelter you can feel it. You're up and down. I had to go outside and find the damage that was done so I had to tell a lie because when I went out there was glass all over the steps, all the tiles were blown off the roofs, glass all down the road and tiles. So I went back and they said 'Oh, what happened?' And I said, 'Not much really' so I had to just, you know, leave it at that. But of course they found out when they went out. Well, my father was profusely thanked by the people that were going to use that shelter they could because we just did not have the warden to keep all these shelters open. From that time, we just, you know, carried on as we were."

Spitfire Production around Shirley Rec during the Second World War

Don Smith (born 1926)
Interviewed 2011

"I left school before the age of 14 and went to work because the War had broken out and my school, Foundry Lane School, was immediately taken over. Within a matter of days it was filled with Canadian troops. I eventually got a job at a place called Auto Metalcraft which is just off of Emsworth Road in a collection of buildings which covered quite an area. It's still there to this day I believe, mostly in small units. At the time I joined that particular place, it was a car works and specialised in car body repairs. In those days you didn't buy bits for car bodies; if they were damaged beyond repair you actually hand-made them so there was basically a lot of skill involved. Possibly, because of that, when the Woolston Works (Supermarine) got bombed in September 1940, work was diversified to wherever they could put it and wherever they could find people that had the skills to be able to produce the requirements for Spitfire building. That is how the factory where I worked came to pick up that particular contract.

We didn't actually build the fuselages or the wings for the aircraft, but what we did do, we built jettison tanks that were special fuel tanks that were fitted to the underside of the aircraft to extend the range of it for Spitfires. We built various air ducts, some of the fuselage panels and we also, at that time, still had a contract for building big fuel tanks for motor torpedo boats and several other things but gradually in the end it basically became work on Spitfires and that continued for quite some time.

Work was diversified all around the area, which is how we came to pick up a contract, but at the same time in Winchester Road, where today you see the modern store of The Range, there was a big garage that had been newly built just before the outbreak of War, Seward's Garage, and that was taken over for Spitfire production. Almost opposite, just to the north of its junction with Wilton Road and Winchester Road was Allom Brothers, which was a lighting firm and that was taken over for Spitfire production. Next door to that was the Sunlight Laundry and that too was taken over for Spitfire production... and just a little further up on the same side was the Hants & Dorset Bus Depot-cum-workshop and that too was taken over for Spitfire production. It was quite surprising in many ways how the production sometimes came down to very small units. Just a little further down Winchester Road just before you get to the junction with St James' Road and St James' Park, there was a big house that stood on the corner, Oatlands House, that was vacated quite some time before the War and was almost derelict, but just behind that was a little garage called Light and Law's. There was just enough room downstairs for a couple of cars and a little rickety wooden staircase that went up the side to a little workshop above. I was on one occasion asked by my foreman at Auto Metalcraft to go up to Light and Law's. I cannot remember what particular reason it was I had to go there, but what I do remember

Don Smith in the back yard of Auto Metalcraft Emsworth Road

when I got there, the chappie working downstairs asked me what I wanted and I said I needed to speak to Mr Law and he said, *'Well he's upstairs on the lathe.'* So, I went upstairs and the man said, *'What do you want son?'* I gave him the message, whatever it was, that I had to give him and he still worked frantically away on his lathe with a great big heap of parts on the floor beside him. He asked me what I was doing at Auto Metalcraft and I told him what we were doing there and so on and, out of curiosity, I asked him what he was doing and he replied.

'Well! Excuse me if I carry on working, I'm making parts for Spitfire propellers and I'm the only one left doing this. If I don't continue then we are not going to win the Battle of Britain!'

So basically that was, you might say, a one-man band."

Shirley Parish Hall and War Work

"Well, the Parish Hall in Shirley (as it is now known) in those days was known as the Rechabite Hall – and the Rechabites were a Christian section of the Church of England.[5] When I first started at our factory, Auto Metalcraft, it employed 30 or 40 people. It expanded as the amount of work increased. Gradually people were induced to receive training in what was Government training centres and there was one at Redbridge and lots of people came from there – young girls as young as 16 and 17, older people were specially trained to come into the factories to work so that possibly, by the time you got to the end of 1941 or so, there was probably something like 400 to 500 people working in that

Don Smith's Memories of Spitfire Production: Sites in Shirley

Editor's Note - The Supermarine Works was extensively damaged by the Luftwaffe on 25th September 1940, after which the Air Ministry ordered that production be dispersed; in Southampton alone, production was later carried out over 28 locations employing about 3,000 people. See here for eight of those locations close to the Park protected by the barrage balloon.

Auto Metalcraft, Emsworth Road

Lowther's Garage, Park Street

Seward's Garage 230

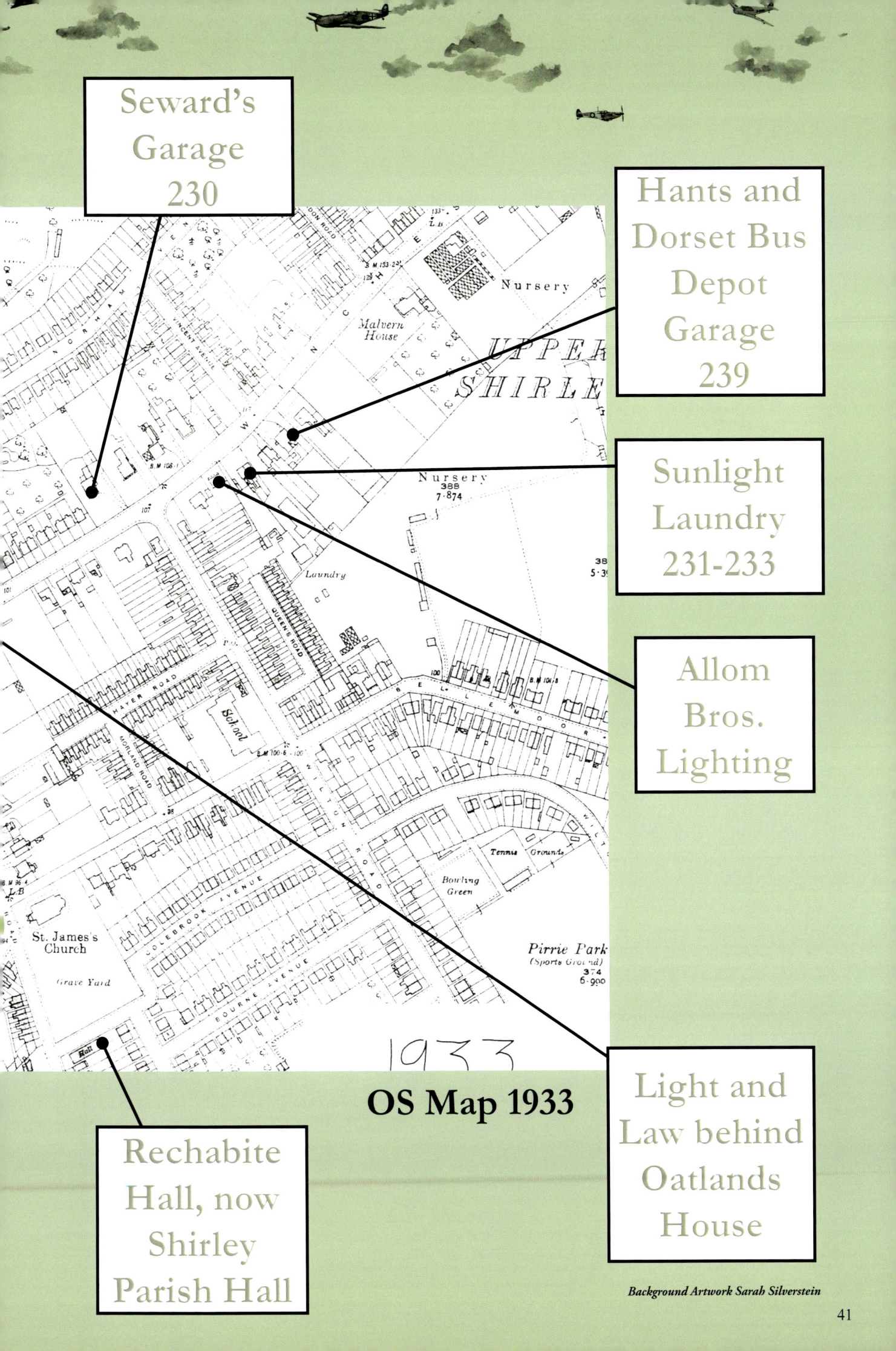

Hants and Dorset Bus Depot Garage 239

Sunlight Laundry 231-233

Allom Bros. Lighting

OS Map 1933

Rechabite Hall, now Shirley Parish Hall

Light and Law behind Oatlands House

Background Artwork Sarah Silverstein

*Workers at Auto Metalcraft
Girls are L-R Pat Pruce, Lily and Nell*

place and as the work expanded they began to look for other areas to use. The company I worked for opened a small satellite factory in premises they found down in Swanwick, and the chaps used to go backwards and forwards to work every day there in an old truck; and they also took over the Rechabite Hall, the Shirley Parish Hall, and I was actually involved in kitting it out with long benches. There was a long bench down the wall each side and a double row of benches right down through the middle. We fitted gas pipes and air blowers underneath the benches so that the girls could sit there on their stools and do brazing work on copper pipes and so on. Obviously, the jettison tanks had pipes in them so that they could be connected to the aircraft fuel systems and a lot of the girls would sit there on their stools at the benches and do the brazing, whatever was necessary, and silver soldering because silver solder being a fairly soft metal, coal gas with air would induce sufficient heat to be able to silver solder but I suppose at one stage there would have been something like about 40 to 50 girls working at the benches in the Rechabite Hall. Their only canteen was down at the far end there was just a little kitchen and they would have a lady that would come in and have a few buns and whatever and make them tea for their tea breaks. So that was the Parish Hall involvement as far as the war effort was concerned. I believe it probably lasted up till the end of the War but I'd left the premises by then or left the factory long since and gone into the Forces myself, so exactly when it closed I can't say. I would think towards the latter part of 1941."

And did you meet some of the girls that used to work there then?

"Oh indeed, yes. One in particular but I met her at the main factory and she didn't work in the Rechabite Hall, she worked in the main factory and she eventually became my first wife. [Ellen (Nell) Sennett]."

Don Smith pictured with Nell 1943 at the back of Auto Metalcraft Emsworth Road

Ellen (Nell) Smith's National Identity Card

Don Smith

42

War Work on Winchester Road

Doreen Couper, née Billows (born 1924)
Interviewed January 2012

"I was born in St Andrews Road and as a child, I moved out then to Chestnut Road, Shirley Warren. I left school at 14 and then went out to work, naturally, because in those days you left school at 14. When the War started you couldn't stay at the job you were in, as they wanted you to go onto War Work. The War came about and I had to either go into the Forces or have a worthwhile job, because by the time you were 18 you had to go into the Forces anyway.

So, I worked at Vickers Armstrong on Winchester Road just past St James' Park. Next door was Sunlight Laundry which turned into the components part of Vickers Armstrong and opposite Seward's Garage was the fuselage department where the fuselages were done - for the Spitfire. Then during the War, I worked further up in that area in the Hants and Dorset - which was the old bus station, for charabancs, as they were called then, now called coaches. They would do all the mending of all the engines and things, you know, inside the coaches and that. And that was the part that I worked in so I knew all of that area beforehand.

I started at Vickers Armstrong, Hants and Dorset Bus Station, at 16 years old. I was head of the Drawings Library and secretary to the foreman of the shop and the senior inspector. That meant I used to do a lot of running about from one place to another! I also helped out with the wages department timesheets and things like that. I went into all the departments that were there with the plans for each department: including the Sunlight Laundry, the components department and Seward's Garage, the fuselage department. I used to go with the drawings from the library to the component department and to Mr Nelson, the head of the whole construction. Mr Nelson's house was alongside the garage; I used to go to his department - it was just him and his secretary in that house. He was involved in all the areas of Vickers Armstrong and Seward's Garage.

In 1942 they had women in Vickers Armstrong, the wing area: they helped build the wings. These were the first women in this area to come into the wing department. I used to go to work at eight o'clock in the morning to half past eight at night then cycle home in the dark. No lights at all were on, nobody was allowed to see a light anywhere and all you had was just two instants to go where you were going.

Course we had a little bit of laughter and fun when we used to go dancing and sometimes - without the sirens we hoped. We'd go to cinemas: there was the Regents Cinema at the top of Shirley, the Rialto and the Atherley next to each other at the middle of Shirley."

When you used to go up to Hants and Dorset to work, do you remember seeing the activity in the Park, the barrage balloon and that then?

"No, not really because it was dark most of the time, you see. Dark in the mornings because you used to sometimes be cycling up there half past seven. During the summer, you didn't sort of look around, you just went on your bike and then coming home it was nearly always dark, because it was half past eight, so you didn't see anything. You know I was lucky enough to work five days a week and a Saturday morning sometimes. If they asked you to work on, you would do it. But when you think of it, a sixteen year old girl, working from eight o'clock until half past eight at night, it's not funny is it?"

Mother's War Effort

Mrs Rita Judd (born 1932)
Interviewed July 2007

"My mother, along with a number of other mothers of young children (mothers with only older children had to work in factories, shops etc.) were asked to take paying guests into their homes. My mother had two young girls from 17-18 years old upwards, for four weeks at a time, who lived with the family and were provided with full board and keep for a certain payment per week, to cover the cost of their care. These girls were trained in engineering skills and then sent off to work in factories around the country. One of the girls was sent to Seward's Garage in Winchester Road, to work on the making of parts towards the assembly of the Spitfire - work which was contracted around many sites throughout Southampton after the Supermarine Works was bombed. She lodged with us for many years, so my mother then continued to have just one of the trainees every four weeks. It seems strange in these days of instant communication, to remember that people rarely spoke about what they did. 'Careless Talk Costs Lives' was a slogan given enormous heed to. Later in the war, a large number of Irish men worked in the city in the Pirelli factory in Southampton. They were also billeted with families."

My War Work at Supermarine, Trowbridge

Vicki Cooper's husband Lesley worked at the Supermarine Factory in Woolston. When it was bombed and work was dispersed, he was moved to Trowbridge in Wiltshire. Vicki found herself also having to undertake War Work at the factory.

Vicki Cooper (born 1920)
Interviewed 2014

"When we went to Trowbridge I had to work in the factory too. I had never worked in a factory in my life... they had to tell me everything, they had to show me what to do. Of course they called Lesley up, you know, they said they were taking too many men from the Spitfire, I mean the women couldn't do all the work... all that work, so he was deferred and I was pleased.

And what did you have to do?

I'd never held a rivet gun before; they had to show me how to do it. I'd never done anything like that in my life. We had to put things on this metal piece, well I don't know what it was mind. But anyway, that's the work I did and, of course, Lesley was a sheet metal worker so he did his work. My friend was worried that we were going to lose the War with me working on the planes."

Spitfire War Work and Dances

Gwendoline Kitchener (born 1915)
Extracts from an interview in 2010

"I was born at 39 Wilton Road, Shirley which was next door to the School and I was one of 11 children – I was the sixth daughter, but my mother lost her first daughter – I attended Shirley School from the age of five till the age of 14 when I left.

My husband was stationed at Calshot. They used to have dances at Calshot and they used to run a bus for the girls from Woolworths and all the shops. I worked at the tobacco factory then, because you couldn't get a job anywhere else and my father was a foreman there. So I got a job there – I quite enjoyed it – it was a nice clean job and we got good money and we used to go to Calshot to the airmen's dances. But my husband played the drums in the orchestra so I didn't get much of a dance – I just sat there. When I said that I was going my eldest sister said to my mother 'You are not going to let her go there are you with all those airmen?' Girls were very sheltered – I mean you didn't know anything.

I had only known him for about eight months – I met him in the November and we were married in the April; I was married at St James' Church. We went to live at Holbury near Calshot and we lodged with a man and a woman – the man worked at the Agri Oil Works as they were then – now it's that great big place [Fawley Refinery]. Mr MacDonald (he was called) – he worked there and we had been married seven months when my husband was posted abroad and of course I went back to my mum. We didn't know where he was going but we were lucky really because he ended up in Rhodesia – he could have gone to Singapore or anywhere like that.

My husband was away for four years during the War. I worked at Vickers, first of all at the top of Wilton Road - there was a big place there and then we went up to Hursley Park and Vickers were there [too]. The men used to make these big templates and we used to stamp them with the numbers on – Bottom Top Londron – parts of the aircraft.

I used to work at Vickers from 8am till 6pm at night – you would come home and have your tea and then go down in the shelter every night – I didn't have much of a social life during the War because my husband was away. We went to the Guildhall and we had a dance – I used to like going to the Guildhall to the Policemen's Balls because they were very nice."

Gwendoline and Ray with bridesmaid Rosina at St James' Church June 1940

"I had this photograph taken for my husband and he carried it all over the world"

5   A Century of Play - 1910s to the 2010s

Play and Play Equipment

Nora Davies (born 1920) shares her memories of playing in the Park:

"My father was Joseph Thursfield Brown and he was working for White Star Line in Liverpool. He was on the Majestic and he was due to go on the Titanic but my mother was expecting my eldest brother. It was due to sail three weeks before my mother was going to have my brother. They asked my father if he would like to wait for another ship so he would be with my mum when Joe, my brother was born. So that's what he did and really, if he hadn't done that, I wouldn't be here (Thanks to Joe)... I used to play in Shirley Rec and had many happy hours there. Also, my children were always at the Rec playing...we used to play tennis in the tennis courts and I think it was about a shilling, something like that. It had banks all round and we used to roll down them as children and we loved it up there. It was really lovely. We did meet a lot of boyfriends up there and well we all came from the same area."

Tennis Courts

"There was a tennis court there (later in the 1930s) and a couple lived in Bellemoor Road – Mr & Mrs Misselbrook – I remember they used to go and play tennis."
Gwendoline Kitchener (born 1915)

"I think there were four grass tennis courts in those days... (the thirties)...the two that are there at present, and two more - closer to Church Street." **Rita Judd**

"The tennis courts backed onto the children's playground which was sort of at the Church corner of the Park. They were on the St James' Road side. I think there were maybe four courts. They were getting a bit run down maybe in the mid-70s but they were still there." **Joan Cook (born 1960)**

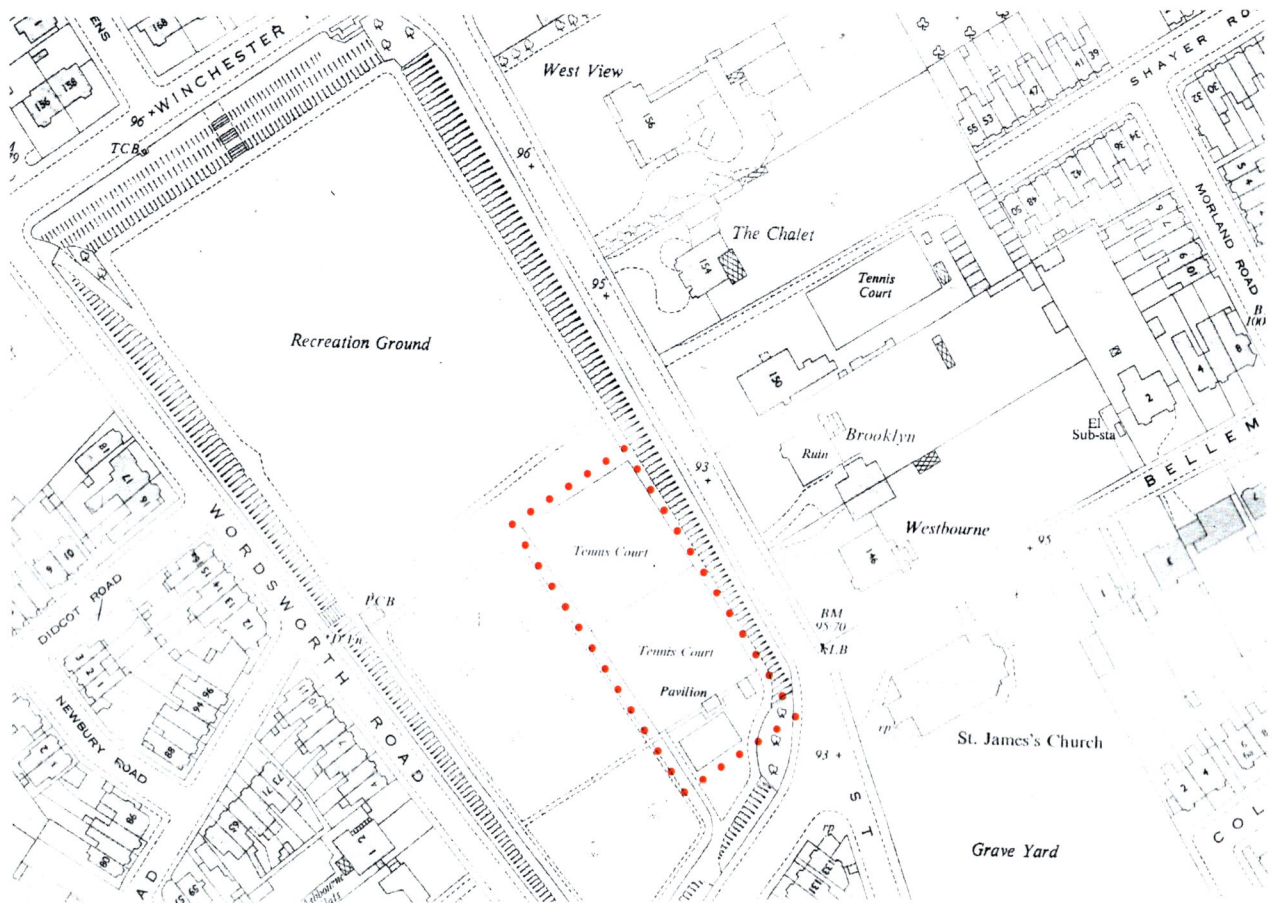

OS Map 1950 – the four tennis courts are visible, as is the main building and the two huts

Norman Burnett - Park Keeper until 1993 remembers:
"We had the two areas of tennis courts which were split into four. We had one hard court and three grass courts which I had to look after. We had the tennis pavilion and the tennis hut next to it. They were both still there when I left."

And were they wooden structures?

"Yes, that's right. The pavilion was just the place where people would get changed for the tennis, you know, just to take their gear off and sit in there if it rained - they'd take a bit of shelter. What I called the tennis hut was really the groundsman's hut, where you take the money. You would sit and watch and make sure that everything was alright when people were playing tennis – that's if you weren't out doing other jobs in the Park. That's where people who worked on the weekend would sit because they wouldn't do anything else, all they'd do is take the money for the tennis."

And that is a job that you would do also, take the money for the tennis?

"Yes. I used to do that as well. I used to have to total the money up at the end of the week - which I used to, thoroughly enjoy doing. Not! Since then - there is only one hard tennis court now (2009) and the grass courts, well, people just played football on them for a kick about or sit on them, don't they?! It's such a shame."

The Playground and the Sandpit

Don Smith (born 1936) recalls: "I have got one little memento of Shirley Rec that I carry with me (and I shall always carry with me). I managed to fall over and get one of the spikes on the fence of the ornamental park through my ear and into the back of my head. I went across to the Children's Hospital which was across the road from the Rec. They patched me up to go home – and that scar's still there now. There was a sandpit just inside of the gates and in front of the tennis courts – roughly about where the café building is now. As kids we saw it as quite a big sandpit. We'd play in there and then we would chuck sand at each other and then we would usually end up having a scrap or something or other. It was on one of those occasions that I'd had some sand chucked at me and I went after the nipper who had thrown it. He ran down the little pathway towards the tennis courts and then turned in sharp left to go into the ornamental garden and I was following him and of course the sand gets chucked about and it was on the asphalt path – and if you can think about it – dry sand on asphalt is very slippery and I ran down and as I turned sharp to go into the park my feet went from under me and I went sideways onto the spikes that were on the fence – and one of the spikes went through my left ear and into my head at the back. It was a bit of a contretemps over the sand thrower and so on and so forth, so I got paid out twice really."

Doreen Couper (born 1924): "My daughter tells me that when they were at school, the banks of St James' Park were much steeper than they are now and they were able to run round the tops of the hills. There weren't swings and roundabouts and things like that in that park. It was just ordinary grass and hilly slopes and grass and flowers and shrubs and trees and the normal park. I think not far off from the 1950s they did a little park area where the children could play - or rather, 1960s shall we say. 1960s would be more like it."

Joan Cook (born 1960) now lives in Nottingham. Joan grew up near St James' Park; she shares:

"We lived in the flat above the National Provincial Bank on the corner of Romsey Road and Anglesea Road. There was a small yard at street level with a bike rack, and metal stairs up to the balcony where the front door was. I don't know how Mum managed to get the pram up the stairs. The Park was halfway between home and school - Shirley Infants - so we spent a lot of time there when I was little. It must have been about maybe 15, 20 minutes' walk, but that's the nearest green space by quite a long way, really. The Park was sort of protected because it's sunken, so once you were down inside it you could run round without easily going onto a road or anything. Then I think maybe parents would sit on the bench and you could, if you were little, go and run around and come back to the benches again. I used to really like running around the slopes at the side, and I remember picking up acorns and oak leaves and things like that. I remember there were other children, sometimes bigger children, on the play equipment that you'd see. So I wasn't sure whether to go on them or not. I remember maybe there were other kids with parents on the next bench and Mum said go and talk to them! So we did meet other kids there. I think because there's a lot of space maybe there were quite a lot of other kids running around the edge of the Park. It's quite spread out so you could have a lot of kids there and not necessarily be altogether. I think you'll be excited about these pictures that my dad (Peter Cook) has fished out, taken by my mum, we think probably in 1964.

I wasn't very clear about the seesaw and this sort of explains why. It's a wooden boat type of thing, with the middle portion that could be sat inside, a raised seat at each end, running boards all along each side and a wooden crossboard with studs on in the middle. You can see quite a bit of detail on [this] photo. I don't remember seeing a similar seesaw anywhere else."

1960s play equipment (see also page 8 photographs) from Joan Cook

Peter Ross in 2012 wrote: "I recently came across the FoSJP webpage quite by accident. I've lived in Southampton all my life (I'm now nearly 57). As a boy we lived in the Regents Park area, King Georges Avenue to be precise, and one of my Grandmothers lived in Hollybrook, so as a young child I would often be taken into Shirley Rec to play, often on a boat shaped ride in the playground."

An Afternoon's Entertainment at the Park

Judy Humby, née Wren (born 1957) wrote in 2014:

L-R Peter Slack, Ivy Doreen Wren, Stephen Slack, Judy Wren - June 1970

"I was thirteen at the time this photograph was taken, and had been living in Shirley Towers for two years. Shirley Rec was very popular and we'd visited it many times from when I was small. As a child there were certain things you had to do in the Park - enter the Park via the Church Street entrance, go down the slope, have a go on the swings, etc, go past the now Café, which was then only toilets, with the Park Keeper's office on the right hand side (to play tennis you had to go and book a time and court). Then climb halfway up the embankment where there was a little track and follow it all the way along to the far end, looking down at the tennis courts and empty half of the Park on the way round, all the way round back to the Church Street entrance and down into the most beautiful part of the Park - the area on the left hand side as you entered via Church Street where every year there was a small avenue of glorious cherry trees and I think roses in the beds. Another play on the swings, etc, and that was an afternoon well spent!"

Sarah Cartwright (born 1964) in 2014 wrote: "When I was a child, my parents used to drive my two sisters and myself into Southampton every fortnight from our home in Hythe. The first stop was Kingsland Market for vegetables, then on to Shirley for the grocery shopping at Sainsbury's. Once the chores were finished, we'd head to Owen's Fish & Chips in Church Street. Mum and Dad would chat to Mr & Mrs Owen while our order was cooked; then it was off up the road to the Park. We had a VW campervan and we'd park up outside St James' Park to eat our fish & chip lunch. Us girls couldn't get the food down fast enough because we knew that, as soon as we were finished, we would be allowed to run down into the Park to the playground. Happy memories!"

"The first photo is one my mum found of the Park itself - I [Sarah Cartwright] think me and my sisters are at least two of the little children running about or on the equipment but I can't be sure. This would have been somewhere between about 1968 and 1974"
[Editor's note – you can just see the hut behind the main building]

"I've enclosed the second pic, which is of all three of us with our dad in Shirley Recreation Ground (I'm the one nearest the camera, aged 12 here) in 1976"

Norman Burnett, the last Park Keeper, remembers SCC staff moving the 1960s play equipment from near the building and creating a new playground in the same position it is in now.

"I know up the St James' Road end they did a lot of work when I was there and a lot of work inside the play areas. They'd changed the play areas around, put bigger play areas in. When I started at the Rec there was still tarmac down on the play area. When they started all these health and safety rules you had to have these rubber surface play areas, so they decided to change the play equipment. When I visited the Park in 2009 the equipment we had put in the Rec between 1987 and 1992 was still there. There were perhaps just a few new smaller bits in there for the younger children. It was still there in 2009, but looking a bit tired."

Children from Shirley Infant School visit the Park to play on the new equipment (estimated as early 1990s)

In 2008, FoSJP Committee members were asked to write to the Heritage Lottery Fund to explain why our Park and playground should be revamped.

This was part of one of the letters that was sent:

"What would our membership say? What have they already said to us? We love St James' Park. We know the play equipment is a bit tired and that the paths just go around the Park and are a bit boring, that access could be better especially for elderly people as there are steep slopes into the Park, that there could be more colour and better planting but despite all this we really do like it (more so since it acquired a toilet and a little kiosk). Why? Because it's a friendly, happy place where people feel safe and there's a sense of community and belonging."

In 2010-2011, St James' Park was to get a brand new playground based on schoolchildren's designs. Just before the play equipment was taken out children from Shirley Junior School shared their own memories of playing on this equipment before it was changed forever in 2011. There were so many wonderful stories and pictures, here are a just few.

I remember when I was younger I used to go and hide in the mini house. I use to get red hands from trying to do monkey bars and I always fell off them on to the tarmac.

I used to play Ice-cream shops in the little wooden house. I used to climb on top of the little house, and on top of the double slide's roof. Stand, or swing in the baby swings, and old big swings. The one thing I do miss, is the raised, hill thing in the middle of the grassy area. But the new park, even though it isn't finished, it is AMAZING!!!!

I remember when there was fair and there was a spitfire and the cubs came down and celebrated! I thought the Spitfire was awesome I had a really good time!

48

Members of St James' Church and local PCSOs gave the Park equipment a lick of paint to help it last a little bit longer

Play equipment in St James' Park 2006-2010

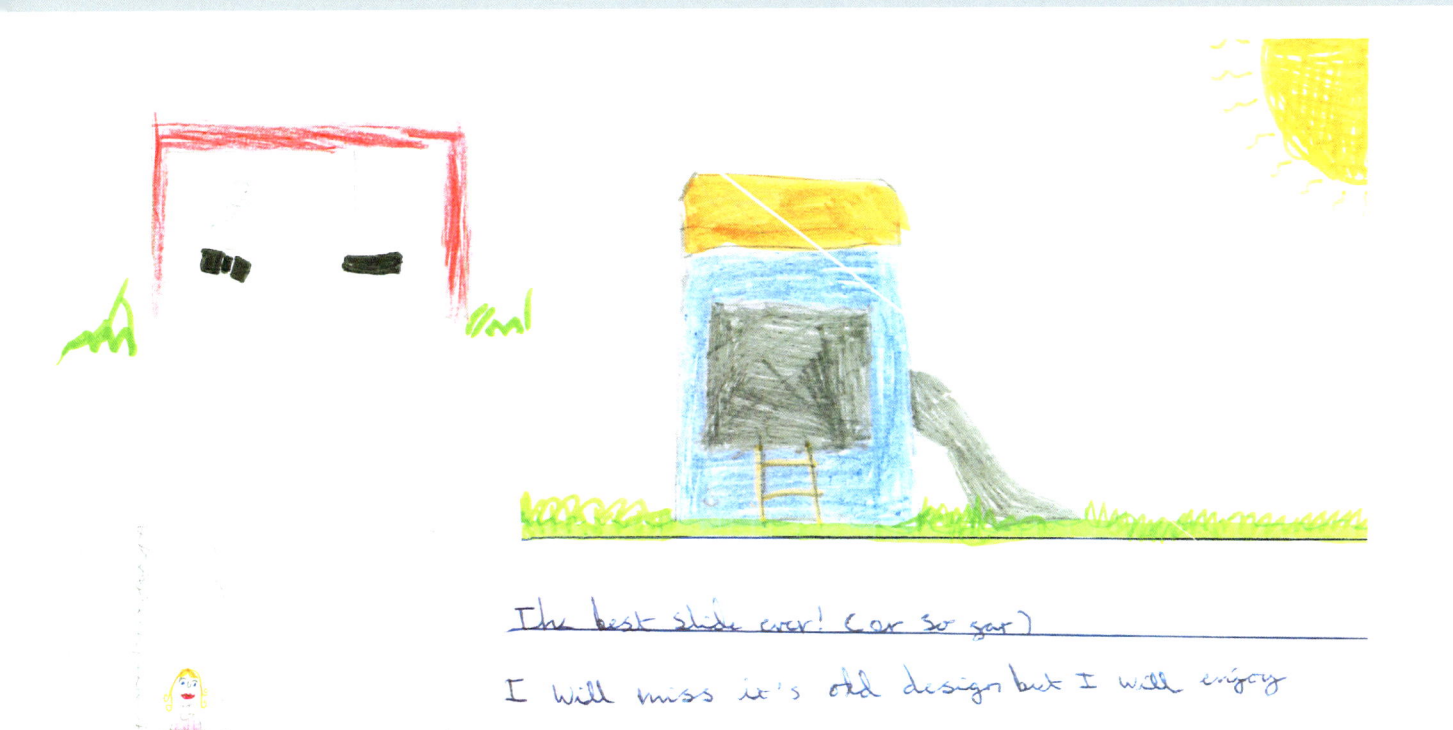

The best slide ever! (or so far)

I will miss it's old design but I will enjoy happily playing in the new design. But I will never lose the happy memories.

I used to jump off the roofs on the Playhouse. I disliked it because tim ran about you ~~~ Ted/Jack

49

When the Park playground was cleared, the old play equipment was piled in a great heap; the roundabout still clearly visible. Many people found that a very sad image to witness: as entwined with that twisted play equipment were years of happy childhood memories. That image inspired this poem that came via the children of Shirley Junior School. It is not certain if it was from a child or an adult, but it certainly captured how many people felt at that time.

"The old Park was there for years...
To see it in a crumpled heap
Made many children start to weep,
The new Park stands
where the old one stood,
I like it a lot, it's very good."

Design Consultant Phil Heaton spoke to the children of Shirley Junior School and asked them to draw the type of play equipment they would like for the new Park. Here are some of their designs (most of them involved climbing and water).

The New Play Equipment 'Imagined'...

50

The New Play Equipment 2011

The New Tennis Courts

before

after

after

after

Former British No.1 Chris Wilkinson with two budding tennis stars of the future at the Park Re-opening Event

In addition to the children's playground, a fitness and sports section has been included in the Park on the site of two of the former tennis courts

The Zipwire

"We were there Sunday afternoon and then again Monday and for a final hour on Tuesday (when I got to ride the zipwire) before they left to go home ... THEY LOVE THE PARK (my grandchildren) - they both get so excited - Thomas was trying to squeeze through the railings as he couldn't wait long enough to go through the gate and down the steps"
Cindy Phillips

Football and Sports Coaching

One of the first games played in Shirley Rec was cricket, but the game that seems to have inspired the most memories is football. These boys pictured in the Park pre-1920, certainly look like they are enjoying a game of 'footy'. There are definite signs of clothing on the ground for goals. Football seems to have inspired many memories from the Park:

"I am Mick Masters, Shirley born and bred, now 70 years old. [2011...] My dad was Tom Masters, born 1887 (a WW1 navy veteran). I have enclosed a picture of him with his football team taken at the Rec about 1910. I do not have any other names for players in the team, but my dad is on the front row, the first one in white, in the left hand corner. (The team were called St Mary's, I have been told they took on that name when the present Saints changed to Southampton from St Mary's.)"

[Editor's note – no records have been checked to verify the team's name]

My dad's football team in Shirley Rec c.1910. Photograph courtesy of Mick Masters

Ken Prior, who works for Southampton City Council's Parks and Open Spaces Team, also has a keen interest in the history of Southampton local league football. Whilst undertaking his research in the Southampton City Archives, he found the following notes from Southampton Council minutes:

On 23rd July 1920 a letter from Shirley Working Men's FC was received, requesting permission to continue playing on Shirley Rec [as St James' Park was then known]; also a letter from the Old Comrades Association for the Church Lads Brigade, applying to play on Saturday afternoons. There was also an application from what appeared to be The Maypole FC for use of the ground on a Wednesday afternoon.

Pictured: Shirley Working Men's F.C. (Southampton City Council Arts & Heritage. Ref M23342)

Judy Humby (née Wren) September 2014: "[This] photograph was taken in 1948/49 and shows a football team (I don't know the name but would like to!) which was run and managed by my father and my uncle. My uncle, Bert Batten, is on the far left of the photo at the back, age 42 years old. My father, Ronald Wren, is on the far right of the photo at the back, age 32 years old. The photo was taken in the left hand side of the Park, as you entered via Church Street, where all the beautiful cherry trees were - there was a row of seats backing onto the tennis courts, facing the trees"

The Old Comrades Association, for the Church Lads Brigade, applied again in 1921. In 1924, when Shirley Working Men's FC applied for permission again, the council response changed to *"the committee cannot guarantee any club the exclusive use of the ground"*. In 1925, their request was turned down with that reason. That policy, of only allowing open use on the open field, and not permitting *'exclusive use of the ground'* for football, is still in force today.

Mrs Rita Judd: "The large grass area at the Winchester Road end of the Park was always used for football and according to Mr. Budd, a friend of mine who is in his eighties, he remembers every other Saturday - League Football being played there by the Shirley Working Men's Club."

Shirley Boys between 1952 and 1958, sitting on the steps of the former Winchester Road entrance to the Park. Lesley's father, believed to be the first on the left in the second row, has since passed away

Sitting on the steps to watch the football is not the only thing that children did; **Gwendoline Kitchener, née Hancock** (born 1915) recalls her childhood in the 1920s: "We used to spend a lot of time at the Recreation Ground - we called it the Recreation Ground then and at one end it had three sets of steps with walls on and I remember that when I was smaller I used to fit in the bottom set of the wall – you could lie on it and my feet would touch the bottom and then gradually as I grew I fitted the second one and then the top one."

Lesley Shotter, née Stapley wrote in 2010:
"Dad used to play a lot of football in St James' Park (or the Rec as it would have been known) and I remember many times watching him from the steps in the picture. His family lived initially in Howard Grove and then in Lumsden Avenue until we moved to Bitterne when I was three years old. My youngest sister seems to think that my uncle Frank, dad's brother, is also in the picture on the right of the same row. He lived in Sir Georges Road, Shirley, until his death. I wondered if anyone had any idea who the other chaps might be or any further history relating to this group?"

Joan Cook (born 1960) and now living in Nottingham, remembers playing on the steps too: "I remember the steps. There's like a brick wall on each side, sloping about 45 degrees downwards. It was red brick at the bottom but on the top of it was sort of curved black bricks - glazed bricks - and they'd get really, really hot. We'd always be tempted to try to slide down but they put several raised bits, about three or four sets of raised bricks part way down the slopes so that you couldn't slide down! But you could slide down the last bit and I think it sort of curved towards the end of the slope. You'd want to try and slide down there but you couldn't really slide very far!"

"On this photo, I'm standing next to one of the benches, dressed in trousers and a sort of furry top with reins on and mittens. There's snow on the ground - it's a very bright winter sun and my hand is held up to shade my eyes from the sun. There's lots of footsteps in the snow and silhouettes of trees and near the bench, which backs onto the tennis courts. Towards the back of the picture there's a low fence and then a hedge and a gap between the fence which leads onto the football field. I think you can see the back of part of the goal post, so I think that's looking across towards the Winchester Road end of the Park, right across the football pitches."

Ken Prior remembers: "From my research I could tell back in the 1920s, there was football played at Shirley Rec, but I've also spoken to people who played football themselves at Shirley Rec in the late 1940s, early 1950s as the team called HMS Dryads used to play there in the Southampton League and obviously, from my research, there's the Shirley Comrades, back in the twenties and thirties. From my own memories which go back to the seventies, working there, I don't think there was organised football at Shirley Rec. People would have played at Shirley Rec on the area which is clearly a football ground sized area but... I don't think there was any sort of real, proper football teams who played there from the seventies onwards, it may have been in the sixties, I don't know. So yes, a lot of football has been played at Shirley Recreation Ground.

I think they would have had nets when they played in the Southampton League in the forties and fifties but I can't really recall any from the seventies onwards. There may have been some goalposts there but certainly not nets and not a properly marked-out pitch. I know in more recent years I've seen teams there just practising going along with their own goal and putting that sort of thing out. Probably these local Tyro League sides, schoolboy sides - you know, children and that they're obviously having some kind of organised training sessions there, but not properly organised football matches, no."

Since the Park has been renovated it has become a popular venue for football and sports related events.

One of the most exciting football related projects to happen in the Park is the Coxford and District Youth and Football Club. Marina Murphy tells us more.

History of the Project

"The Coxford and District Youth Project (CDYP) began in 1990 with no funds, equipment or paid workers. It is an independent registered charity which is truly community-led. For nearly 20 years it offered a wide range of activities, support and information & advice to young people. For various reasons funding for the project has dwindled over the last two years and CDYP was at the point of shutting it down."

[Editor's note: The project has had a revival since it moved to St James' Park – it has been supported by the ParkLife Café, in St James' Park, a Community Interest Company, whose profits go back into serving the community.]

"The young people that attend the training are taking part in a positive and healthy activity. Some of them are from vulnerable and disadvantaged backgrounds and are being provided with a positive diversionary activity as well as raising their self-esteem and aspirations. Many of these young people would find it very difficult to join a mainstream football team due to lack of money, lack of support from their parents, transport, aspirations but primarily because they would not 'fit in' and be accepted because of their disabilities or behaviour. Having said this there are a handful of able bodied young people who attend as well, including one girl. This is of benefit for both groups of young people ie having positive role models for those that are disadvantaged and helping the able bodied to accept those that are different to them and with whom they would not normally mix.

Three of the young boys have been able to register for Tyro League football teams through gaining confidence and experience in this team and through the project paying their signing up fees which they would not have been able to afford themselves.

Football sessions have been running regularly on Tuesday afternoons and during school holidays as funds allow us. We have managed to scrape together the funding and voluntary support to keep the project going since October 2012."

"It is very important to provide regular activities for these young people who often do not have consistency or stability in their lives."

Sports Coaching in St James' Park

Prior to the renovations of 2010-2011, St James' Park did not host regular sports coaching for children. Since the improvement to facilities the Park has become a popular venue for sports related events.

Football Skill Practice at the Play in the Park Re-opening Event 16th July 2011

Football practice at FoSJP events prior to 2010/11

Also starting in 2012, local sports coaching company, Team Spirit, ran a series of football coaching workshops

Community Games

Seeing the benefits that sport and team sports can bring into children's lives, Marina Murphy, FoSJP's Community Volunteer Coordinator organised a Community Games event in July 2014. Marina writes:

"Inspired by the London 2012 Olympic Games, the Community Games was a two-day event organised by FoSJP with help from the Southampton City District Scouts to bring the local community together to take part in sporting and cultural activities at St James' Park.

We were delighted to host two special guests - the event was officially opened on Saturday by Olympic silver medallist diver Peter Waterfield, and was officially closed on Sunday by Great Britain Wheelchair Rugby player and London 2012 Paralympic athlete Aaron Phipps - both local heroes from Southampton!

The many sports and activities on offer included arts and crafts, athletics, badminton, basketball, boccia, boxing, a climbing wall, cycling ramps & agility, dodgeball, face painting, fencing, football challenges, golf, handball, henna tattoos, giant Jenga, martial arts, a maze, a minithon, rugby skills, old school games, a skipping workshop, a street art workshop, volleyball and yoga - something for everyone!

Visitors were entertained by a blues/folk band, a brass band, cheerleaders, a choir, a mad scientist, and a saxophone group, and were kept refreshed by the ParkLife Café, food stalls from different countries, and of course a Tea Tent!

Many stalls were present including the Bike Doctor, British Sign Language, the Rose Road Association, and a lucky dip. A raffle, with many prizes generously donated by local organisations, and a tombola together raised almost £1,300 to go towards funding future community activities in and around the Park."

Following on from our Community Games event in July 2014, one of our volunteers, Scott, could see the potential of St James' Park for the benefit for young people. His idea became a reality when four other volunteers from the event agreed to get involved.

Scott and his team were also being helped out by Tom and Beth who run District Sports in Winchester, providing grass roots coaching in a multitude of sporting activities to primary schools throughout the region. Tom and Beth volunteered at our Community Games event, and have also volunteered for this project as they are community minded and happy to share their skills and knowledge.

Youth Sports & Games Club

For ages 6-12
Dress appropriately for rain or shine!

Every alternate Saturday from 18th October 2014
10.30am—12.30pm
Outside the ParkLife Café, St.James' Park

FREE but a 50p donation would be much appreciated!
No fizzy drinks, please

funded by
heritage lottery fund
LOTTERY FUNDED

run by
FoSJP
Friends of St.James' Park

6 In Need of a Friend

The Establishment of FoSJP
Nichola Caveney

It was a beautiful June day. My husband Martin and I sat in the afternoon sun enjoying a cup of tea whilst our daughters aged 5 and 7 played in the playground. The park was busy with a relaxed, laid back atmosphere. Parents chatted, children ran around laughing and all was good with the world. On our return to our home in Shirley, Southampton, we passed our local green space – St James' Park. Why couldn't our local park be as good as the one we had just travelled 10 kilometres to visit in Romsey?

Martin and I were married in St James' Church, Shirley in 1993 and moved into our house near St James' Park six months later. We loved the area for its convenience; and over the years built up strong relationships with friends from work, The Maskers (a local amateur dramatics group) and most especially with others who worshipped at our local parish church, St James'.

We seldom went into St James' Park until our first daughter was born in 1997. I vividly remember getting ready to take my newborn baby out for her first walk in the pram. I bundled her up against the cold November winds and proudly walked down to the Park. One lap around the perimeter path within the Park was enough and then we headed the short distance home again! Over the years, the Park was a useful place to meet other mums whilst our children played in the little playhouse presenting us with pretend ice creams through the window, slid down the slide, and tried their best to swing from the monkey bars! It was only after that visit to Romsey Memorial Park that I realised how much better St James' Park could be. What a difference it would make if we could have somewhere to get a hot drink to help while away the hours. How much more convenient would it be to be able to take our children to the toilet when they needed it, instead of squatting them in the bushes?

Play equipment in the Park 2003

By June 2005, Martin and I had for some time been part of a church 'Cell Group'. This was a group of 8-10 people who met once a week to pray and learn more about God's word. We had become good friends and had a lot in common, with children of similar ages. The week after our visit to Romsey, I mentioned in passing what a pleasant experience visiting the Memorial Park had been. Mike Smith, one of the cell members, immediately felt it was an opportunity we could take in St James' Park, suggesting we could take the abandoned toilet block (that was situated at one end of the Park), and re-open it as a coffee shop. The whole cell were in agreement that this would be a great project and were very excited about the prospect of making a difference.

'The seed was planted. The dream was dreamt'

A month later, I had a chance encounter with an acquaintance, Tim Davies who worked at Southampton City Council. I mentioned the toilet block/coffee shop idea to him and he thought it sounded quite plausible and said he would get a name and contact number. This turned out to be Jon Dyer-Slade, who was then Parks and Open Spaces Manager in Southampton. On July 26th 2005, I had my first meeting with Jon, Paul Fulford (Landscape and Development Officer) and David and Helen Hazlewood (the Vicar of

Baby's Outing to the Park – Catherine Struthers with Anne 1960

St James' Church and his wife). We met in the Park and discussed our idea of developing the toilet block into a coffee shop. It was then that Jon suggested that the best way forward would be to look at how we could improve the whole Park, rather than the building in isolation. He suggested we consider forming a 'Friends' group…

Looking back, I guess this initial meeting was pretty significant in many ways. It was the first step in my personal journey with the Park which lasts to this day. It was also the beginning of a professional relationship with Jon from whom I have learnt so much and have such admiration. Southampton City Council are so lucky to have a man of vision, wisdom and skill working for them for, without a doubt, the Park in its present form would not be there were it not for him.

Over the following months, with the full support of our Cell Group, I made contact with all sorts of people and organisations within the Council that I never even knew existed! Almost all were very supportive and helpful; however, there were some who were cynical. I remember going to a Neighbourhood Renewal Strategy meeting in Shirley Towers where action plans were discussed and the need for a quality community space mentioned. I outlined our proposals to the meeting and was challenged by a local councillor who was pessimistic that the plan could work as the costs would be too high and vandalism too great a risk. Years later, our optimism won through, as that same councillor would officially re-open the Park!

By Christmas 2005, a way forward had been agreed. We would set up a group known as the Friends of St James' Park (FoSJP), with a formal constitution and a bank account (into which St James' Church, and Churches Together in Shirley (CTIS) each gave £100). There were some concerns about opening up the building as a café, so it was decided that in the short term we would re-open a toilet and start with a kiosk to show there was a demand for refreshments. From there, we would look into opening up the rest of the building as a community space/café. After that, our long term aim was from 2007 to look at the development of the whole Park.

Throughout January 2006, the members of our cell group worked on the establishment of the Friends Group, with its aim being 'To maintain and improve the physical and natural environment of the Park in liaison with Southampton City Council'. The membership was (and is) open to anyone interested in actively furthering the purposes of the Group. It is important to be clear that although the original group was founded by members of a church, they agreed that FoSJP itself should not be a Christian organisation. It is a group set up for the whole community regardless of age, race, sex or religion, and this has always been a fundamental objective.

On January 26th 2006, a constitution was signed, and FoSJP was born. I think it only right to mention by name those who signed this, as these were the original committee members and those who had that initial seed of an idea and gave birth to the Friends of St James' Park.

'Nichola and Martin Caveney, Trudie and Mike Smith, Sophie and Johnny Carrington, Theresa Bowen, Victoria Horne, Casey Sewell.'

I was honoured to be the chair of the group.

All of these people have invested many hours of time and energy to see the Park become what it has today. Indeed several of them still have very active roles within the life of the Park.

It was around this same time that I had another meeting with Jon to talk about the building design and the schedules of work. Then he dropped the bombshell. He told me there was a new lottery fund specifically for parks, named 'Parks for People'. He suggested we apply for ONE MILLION POUNDS from the Heritage Lottery Fund (HLF)! Suddenly a group of friends chatting about how we'd like to get a cuppa in a park was turning into something really serious.

Some advice for anyone ever thinking of applying for a lottery grant: you will need a lot of patience and a huge amount of time as the process has many stages with lots of research, consultation and justification! The first step was the pre-application advice stage where we submitted general ideas to the HLF. They gave feedback that it was the sort of project they would support, so we then had to apply for a Project Planning Grant. This awarded us the funding we needed to employ consultants to help us apply for the main application grant! The whole process, from the initial pre-application to the Park's restoration took five years! Thank goodness the council, very ably led by Helen Saward, took the lead on this process.

The FoSJP committee realised that they needed to 'launch' the group and quickly gauge support for the lottery project idea, so we organised our first promotional event on 30th April 2006 alongside SCC and St James' Church called 'The Noise'. The aim of this event was to invite people to join FoSJP and to ask visitors to complete a questionnaire to find out what they used the Park for and what their priorities would be for the Park's future. Over 400 questionnaires were completed and many people became members. In addition to this, some teenagers and adults from the local church set about cleaning and painting the toilet block (which hadn't been used for years) in preparation for its re-opening.

I guess it was around about this time that I realised how important the Park was to the local area. How much it was loved despite its rather sad demeanour. This realisation was reinforced in July 2006 when we were presented with a Southampton Green Spaces Award for the 'Best Community Park' (as nominated by local residents). We knew we had a long way to go, but it was exciting and motivating to know that this really was something the community were behind.

So, work started apace to transform the dilapidated toilet block into a kiosk. The Council found funds to remove the urinals (we were basing the kiosk in what used to be the men's public toilets!), and put in a sink, work surfaces, cupboards, a stable door and a shutter. We received two individual donations totalling £1,500 which enabled us to get appropriate flooring laid and buy equipment such as an urn, fridge and freezer. We decided to run

The Kiosk opens for business run by a team of dedicated volunteers

the kiosk with volunteers serving hot and cold drinks, crisps, chocolate bars, muffins and most popular of all…ice poles!

After much hard work by the Council and FoSJP, the Kiosk (and toilet) opened for business at 1.30pm on 9th August 2006. We had printed off 200 vouchers worth 50p each which we handed out to those in the Park which was a great way of talking to people about what we were doing. The Southern Daily Echo came and I was filmed for their website and also spoke to a reporter on the phone. The main people we were working with at the council came along: Jon and Helen, along with Hilary from the Hawthorns Centre and Stuart, the area coordinator (who continues to work closely with FoSJP's Gardening Team and has been so supportive over the years). The sun shone and there was such a lovely happy atmosphere - we were thrilled that the first part of our dream was being realised one year on from its conception. By the end of the day, we had taken £133!

We organised several more events in the months that followed, but the one that stands out most in my mind was a spring bulb planting session that we ran with help from SCC's Adrian Crook at the end of October 2006. We invited FoSJP members and the local community to come down to the Park to help plant over 1,000 daffodil, tulip, crocus, and snowdrop bulbs in the Park. A lady I didn't recognise turned up, armed with a bag of particularly beautiful tulip bulbs. She told me she lived in some flats by the Park and didn't have a garden. She wanted to plant the bulbs in memory of her son who had recently died.

Now that we were a constituted community group (though never a charity), it opened up the opportunity of applying for grants. This may sound ungrateful, but over the next few years, we were so successful when applying for funding, we had to stop asking for anything more as we didn't have the capacity to spend it!

The first big success we had was when St James' Park was chosen from over 200 applicants to represent the South region in Park It! 2007. This was a national programme of events organised by GreenSpace over that summer which aimed to encourage people to discover the history of their parks and to celebrate their significance in the local community. We were awarded a grant of £10,000 (funded by the Heritage Lottery Fund) and more importantly, given support and advice by both the Park It! team and SCC on how to put on a large scale event. We decided to call our event Park100 to celebrate the fact that it was 100 years since St James' Park was first purchased for use as a recreation ground.

We chose July 7th as the date to put on Park100, and I think it was about six months before then that we had our first planning meeting. We decided to run the event from 12 noon to 9pm, with a mixture of stalls (non-commercial), entertainment, and refreshments. The committee sprang into action with everybody helping to set up subcommittees to organise the different areas. I learnt so much that summer about event management, and in hindsight it was very fortunate that I was only working part-time as Park100 took over my life!

Park100 7th July 2007

Summer 2007 was exceptionally wet, and as July 7th approached, all those involved were getting more and more concerned about the state of the soggy grass, and how bad weather would impact on all that we had organised. However, miraculously, the sun shone for the five days before the event, drying up the ground and July 7th 2007 dawned bright and hot.

A magnificent replica Spitfire took pride of place in the middle of the Park, with stalls run by local charities, groups, and societies running around the perimeter path. At one end of the field was a stage showcasing the music and dance talents of local schools and clubs, with local bands invited to perform from 6pm into the evening. We had various vintage fairground rides, bouncy castles and a moving climbing wall to entertain younger visitors, whilst adults enjoyed browsing the history stalls and learning more about the history of the Park. The refreshment team boldly decided to get volunteers to provide almost all the refreshments and what an army they recruited! They served hot and cold drinks, burgers and sausages, hot potatoes, vegetable samosas, strawberries and cream, cakes and ice-creams!

It was a fantastic day of fun events and entertainment, provided by the people of Shirley for the people of Shirley and beyond. An estimated 10,000 people passed through the gates to take part, and over 200 volunteers were recruited to help on the day. The number of volunteer hours spent arranging the event must have been well in excess of 1,000. It was exhausting and exhilarating in equal measures, and all those involved learnt so much about putting on an event and felt a great sense of achievement. This comment sums up the feedback we received:

"What a wonderful afternoon it was, it was ever so busy. We really thought it was excellent. There were a variety of things to do, there were children enjoying themselves, and there was a nice cup of tea. Well done."

Now FoSJP had categories for events: large (1,000+ people), medium (500-1,000 people), and small (less than 500 people). We knew we were unlikely to have the time, energy, or money to put on another large scale event in the near future, so over the next few years we concentrated on putting on regular small and medium scale events. We tried hard to choose events which would appeal to different interests, but inevitably they were almost all aimed at families who used the Park. After the enormous task of organising Park100, these events were relatively easy to run and generally free to those who took part (thanks to profits made in the kiosk).

Whilst we continued to organise the volunteer-run kiosk, put on events and encourage the diversity of wildlife in the Park, a team of us were hard at work preparing the bid for the lottery grant. As we were applying for funding from the Heritage Lottery Fund, the history of the Park was always a key component of our bid. We were extremely lucky to have Michaela Lawler-Levene on the FoSJP Committee who was initially invited in 2006 to be FoSJP's Press Officer. As well as promoting the Park100 event she organised several of our BBC Breathing Places wildflower planting events in the Park. Because the previous FoSJP History Coordinator, Johnny Carrington, was busy with stage management in the Park100 event, Michaela also produced a history display for the centenary. This fostered a real passion for Shirley's local history and since then Michaela has done a remarkable job bringing together the different aspects of the area's past. She has had to use real detective skills tracking down maps, photographs and documents relevant to the Park, as well as interviewing people and recording oral history. She has built up a team of enthusiastic and valued volunteers who together have represented FoSJP at numerous conferences and fairs, as well as organising several series of free history talks. This book is just one strand of the fantastic job that she has done as part of the pre- and post-funding process.

As well as making a case for the importance of researching the history of the Park, in the lottery bid, we also had to prove that there was a desire and a need for updated facilities in the Park, including a community café. In April 2009, I attended a one day course called 'So you want to run a Community Café?' run by the Development Trust Association (DTA) and the Sunlight Development Trust. I went with Sophie Carrington and Victoria Horne (who also happens to be my sister!) as they were the kiosk managers, and also had a strong vision about how a café in the Park might operate. The course was both inspirational and challenging. We learnt about what a community café is, the various business models a community café can use, how to make a community café engaging and viable, how volunteers can be used, and much more. We were also taught the importance of research and that was our next step.

I would like to point out at this stage that in 2009, the only other coffee shops/cafés (of the style that we were considering) in the Shirley area were Poppy's, on Shirley High Street, and The Range's in-store café, about half a mile away from the Park. Now, as I write this in November 2014, I can count at least 10 within a one mile radius of the Park. Little did we know then what a resurgence of coffee shops (and competition) there was to come…

So, back in 2009, extensive research by a number of people helped us to develop a plan for the type of café we hoped we could provide. Local resident Rebecca Kinge had by now joined the Committee with the role of overseeing the restructuring of the kiosk to a café. She worked tirelessly, researching possible business models, applying for grants, meeting catering consultants and learning as much as she could about the industry. Together with Sophie Carrington's experience and vision, and Mike Smith's business expertise and experience of working with social enterprises, we were confident that a café in the Park had a viable future.

In October 2009, I remember I had just parked my car on my way to visiting my sister when I received a call from Helen Saward to say she had received the news we had been waiting for - we had been awarded the stage 2 pass and grant of £1,102,000 to implement all the plans we had submitted to the HLF. It was all systems go!

Waiting for the decision

We got the grant!

From the outset, the lottery bid, although coordinated by SCC, was a partnership with FoSJP. As such, in my capacity as FoSJP Chair, I was heavily involved in all aspects of the development process. In the months that followed the Stage 2 award, I quickly learnt about the tendering process, project board meetings, dealing with architects, the construction industry, and much more. At times, I did feel a heavy responsibility to represent the community I am part of, but it was incredibly exciting to be part of the creation of a brand new park.

Making decisions on a weekly basis about different aspects of the Park (from the positioning of benches to choosing the size of the holes on the gazebo structure) became a regular feature of my life. There are a couple of things though that really stand out for me. The first was travelling to a quarry on Ham Hill in Somerset with Project Manager Helen Saward from SCC. In the architectural designs, large boulders from this quarry were to be dotted around the new playground. Various boulders were lined up at the mouth of the quarry for us to 'inspect'. I have to admit now, one boulder looks much like another after a while, so Helen and I chose about 10 and instructed the quarry to choose the rest on our behalf!

The other thing I still look at with pride is the inscription on the floor in the centre of the Park. I felt that there needed some sort of feature at the 'crossroads' in the Park, and I can't remember when or why, but for some reason I had the idea of inscribing the chorus from Blur's song Parklife there. After gaining EMI's kind permission to use the line (gratis) I then had to track down a stonemason who could take on the job. Unfortunately, most stonemasons aren't willing (or capable) of taking on this sort of commission as it was so large, so I was lucky to find one in Chichester. He was able to reproduce my design and I took a trip to his workshop to see it being created before watching it being gingerly lowered into position in the Park.

Work to develop St James' Park began in July 2010, and as the time approached for it to re-open almost exactly one year later, there was a flurry of activity getting the café ready to open. Unfortunately, we had underestimated the cost of fitting out the café, and there was a shortfall of £20,000... A chance encounter with someone at a party resulted in a very generous grant from DP World who run the container port in Southampton! At this time, FoSJP decided we didn't have the capacity to run the café as a business, so we founded a community interest company called ParkLife (named after the song!) to run the café and community room as a social enterprise. A team of valiant volunteer directors were chosen to oversee this, on the understanding that any surplus profits made by ParkLife would be given to FoSJP who would use the money to further improve park facilities and services for the community.

On Wednesday July 6th, 2011, St James' Park in its new form opened to the public. We opted for a 'soft opening', meaning we didn't advertise the fact that the barriers would finally be taken down on that day. Word soon spread however as children, who had been gazing longingly though the Heras fencing for weeks, poured out of the local schools. The Park was soon packed with happy excited children and parents as months and years of planning had finally been realised.

'The dream had finally come true'

There have been so many people involved in the project over the years that it is difficult to acknowledge everybody, and I am sure I have forgotten some key contributors to the process. Please accept my apologies now if I have not mentioned you. There is, however, one other person who merits particular thanks and that is Martin Gardner. In 2006, I naively asked Martin if he would consider setting up a website for FoSJP. Little did either of us know how much of Martin's time and effort this was going to take over the subsequent years. As I write, the website has had over

"Helen and I went to the quarry to choose the stones - all 100 of them!"

63

Before

Before

After

64

37,000 'hits', and is not only a place to find out about what is going on in the Park, but is also an accurate record of all the events and changes that have happened in the Park since FoSJP's creation. It is an amazing reference tool for those wanting to know about the history of the Park and its surrounding area, and also contains a wealth of information about environmental aspects of the Park - both natural and manmade. Martin joined the FoSJP Committee in 2009 and also had a vital role during the construction works. All in all, his contribution to the Park's success cannot be underestimated.

Another person to mention is one of the original committee members who is still in post as Treasurer of FoSJP: Theresa Bowen. She has been a real 'Friend' to the Park these past eight years. I am personally grateful for her friendship and efficient administrative support. She has been the backbone of FoSJP and I appreciate and acknowledge everything she has done for FoSJP and the local community. I would also like to thank Theresa's employers the Shirley Parish Church for their continued support throughout this project and in particular the Rev. David Hazlewood, the Rev. Dan Clark and the many parishioners who gave their time helping at the early FoSJP events.

I hope that FoSJP's story inspires others to make differences in their own community. We were just a group of individuals who had a simple idea, and with a bit of dogged determination and a lot of support from our community, realised our vision - and more - in the end. Southampton City Council has been amazing throughout this process, and as well as providing at least 25% match funding, have themselves shown vision and commitment to a local community.

Finally, I need to pay homage to my husband Martin and my daughters for putting up with the hours I have spent involved with FoSJP and in the Park. My children, who were just 5 and 7 when we started the process, are now 14 and 17, and are more likely to meet their friends in the café for a drink than play on the apparatus! The last eight years have been an amazing journey for me personally, and I consider myself very lucky to have worked with dedicated, professional, enthusiastic individuals, on a project which has made such a difference. Together, I believe we have created a Park that our community will enjoy for years to come.

Enjoying a cup of coffee at the new café

The Lottery Grant Restoration and Renovation
Helen Saward, Project Manager, Southampton City Council

In 2006, a small group of local residents approached Southampton City Council with the aim of improving the Park for the local community by re-opening the toilets and creating a small kiosk facility. The group quickly became the Friends of St James' Park with over 450 members, and they continue to be one of the most successful community groups of its type in Southampton. At around the same time the 'Parks for People' programme started, funded by the Heritage Lottery Fund and Big Lottery; St James' Park seemed to meet all the criteria. After several years of planning, consultation and applications in October 2009 we finally had the news that we were successful in securing a grant that with match funding from the Council and FoSJP totalled a project budget of £1.7 million.

The lottery grant was spent on a wide range of physical improvements within the Park and also on audience development activities, heritage activities, events and training aiming to engage the wider community. The Park now really has something for everyone thanks to the restoration and refurbishment which was completed in July 2011. Works included creating new welcoming entrances, an adventurous children's play area, climbing wall and basketball area, outdoor gym equipment and two new purpose-built tennis courts. There are also new walkways with planting and wildlife areas and bird and bat boxes. St James' Park is one of the only public spaces in Southampton to have renewable energy in the form of PV cells which you can see mounted on the gazebo in the centre of the Park.

Energy-Saving Measures in St James' Park
Martin Gardner

Several of the design elements of the improvement works focused on energy conservation; we hope that this will reduce the environmental footprint of St James' Park and provide educational activities for local schoolchildren.

Air Source Heat Pump

Rather than using a conventional gas-powered water boiler to heat radiators, the café building is heated via an external air source heat pump.

The air source heat pump extracts low grade thermal energy (at ambient temperature) from the environment (i.e. heat freely available in the outside air), upgrades the heat to a higher temperature, and via an internal heat exchanger releases that heat into water running through underfloor pipes throughout the building. The underfloor pipes are used to divide the building into seven heating zones, each of which can be separately temperature-controlled. The energy efficiency of this system is estimated at up to 300% i.e. for every 1 kW of energy spent on running the system - pumping air and water around, upgrading heat - up to 4 kW of thermal energy can be extracted from the environment, giving 3 kW of surplus energy for heating the building.

Photovoltaic Cells

St James' Park is now one of a very few public spaces in Southampton to have renewable energy in the form of photovoltaic (PV) cells found on the top of the Gazebo at the end of the Botanical Walk which is designed to accommodate the cells at the optimum angle for their operation. The Gazebo has an array of 12 PV cell modules, which can produce up to nearly 3 kW of electricity. Underground ducting takes generated electricity back to the building, where it can either be used to reduce local energy usage or fed back into the national grid under a Feed In Tariff scheme to provide additional income for ParkLife, the community interest company set up by FoSJP to operate the ParkLife Community Café as a social enterprise.

The team of FoSJP volunteers have dedicated their free time to arranging community events, promoting the Park and involving the local community in all aspects of park life. This project is a great example of close working links between the local community, FoSJP and the City Council which has enabled the Park to be transformed and will continue to help develop the Park to meet the needs of the local community into the future. Nichola Caveney was a founding member of FoSJP and was the driving force behind the project, representing the local community and ensuring users views were at the forefront of the project. Nichola was chair of the Friends group from its inception in 2006 until 2012 and dedicated hundreds, if not thousands of hours of her time to support the project. She has been a great ambassador not only for the Park, but also for volunteering in the community and for working in genuine partnership with the City Council to make improvements.

Since 2009, the Council has faced a difficult financial position and the service area supporting parks across the city has faced budget cuts of around 40% (to 2014). One of the biggest challenges we faced was managing this improvement project with reducing maintenance budgets - therefore it was vital that the Park was designed with sustainability and low maintenance in mind. The work of FoSJP and its Gardening Team have been and will continue to be important to the future success of the Park. The Park won its first Green Flag in 2012 and continues to achieve this high standard. With the continued support of the local community we expect the Park to go from strength to strength. St James' Park went on to retain the coveted Green Flag award in 2013 and 2014.

Café Kitchen Heat Exchanger

In the café kitchen, large amounts of fresh air need to be supplied to replace air that is extracted to counteract the effects of a full range of kitchen equipment - a six burner range, deep fat fryer, grills, etc. - all being used at once. Up to 0.76 m³ per second of air needs to be exchanged and on cold days this supplied air needs to be heated up to internal temperatures to avoid excessive draughts in the kitchen and the café. To warm this large amount of air with the least amount of energy a Full Heat Recovery unit has been installed. This works to recover all heat from the extracted air to warm up the air being supplied into the kitchen area thus no energy is needed to heat this supplied air. Some energy is required to drive the electric fans that supply and extract the large volumes of air required. The full heat recovery unit is large in order to maximize the surface area shared between the outgoing used air and the supplied fresh air, so that as much heat as possible gets transferred to the supplied air and is installed outside the kitchen wall.

Roof-Lights

Electrical lighting needs in the ParkLife Building have been significantly reduced by the five large roof-lights. These were designed to be representative of World War II searchlights. The roof-light design uses thermally efficient double glazing retaining a basic 'inverted searchlight' shape and providing improved light efficiency. During the daytime, no electric light is needed in the rooms below these roof lights including the Community Room.

Windows
The café area has large areas of double glazing which both keep heat in and let light in, reducing both heating and lighting energy needs.

Masterplan

The Renovation Process

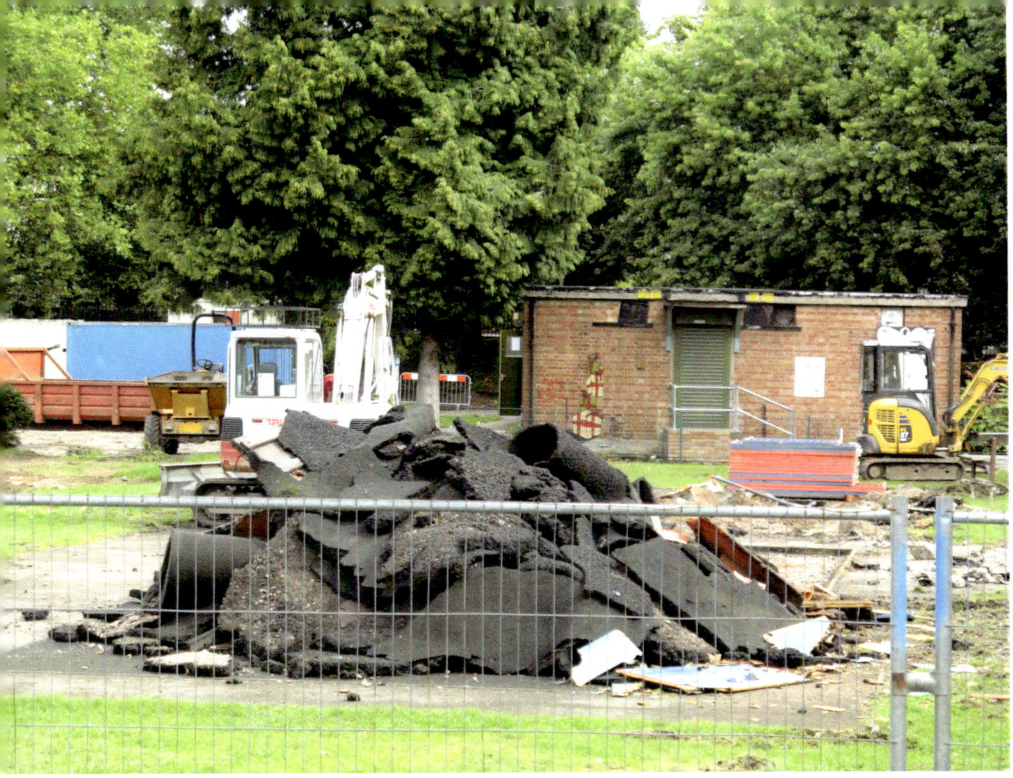
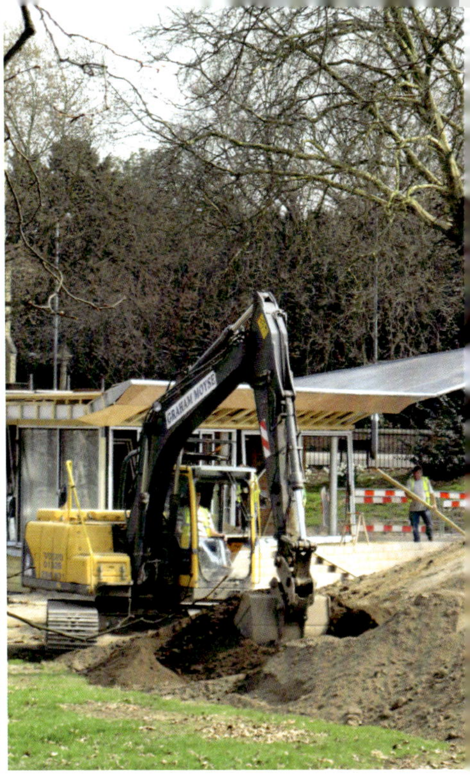
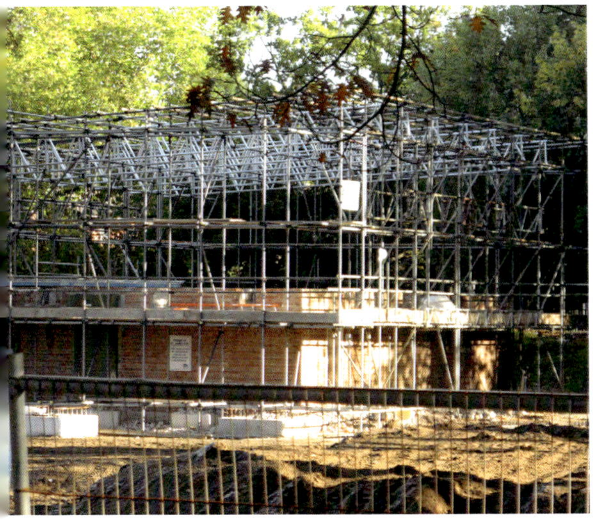
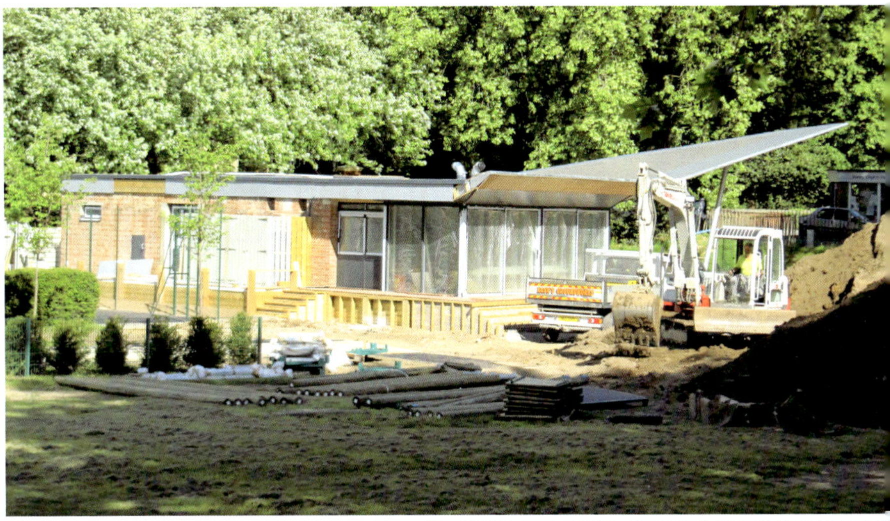
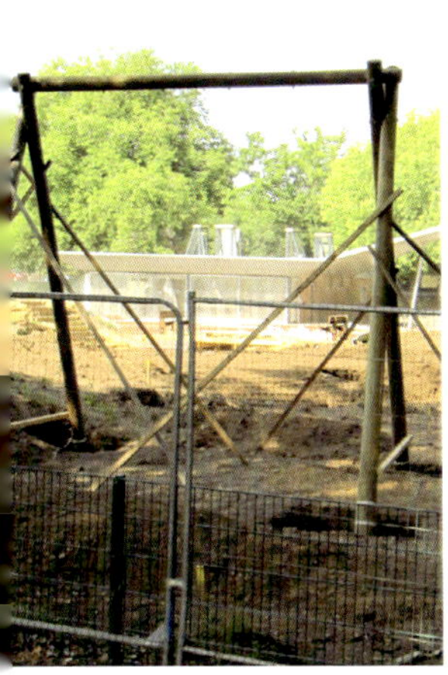
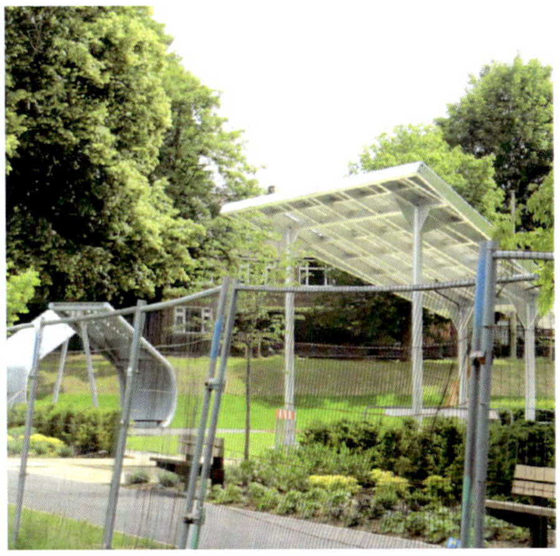
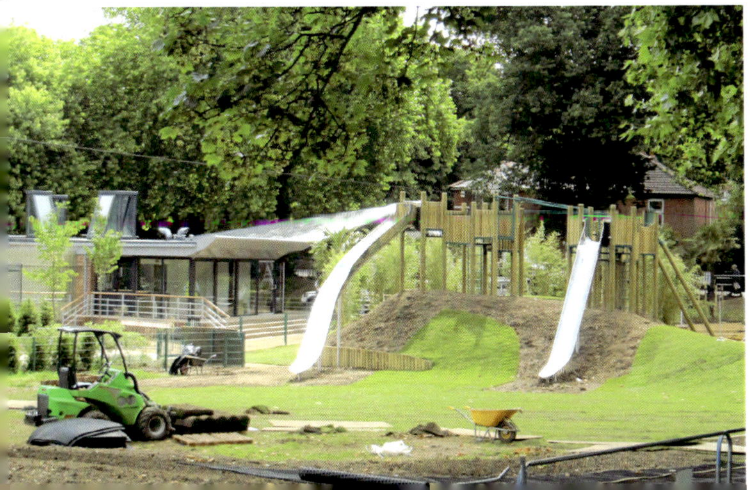
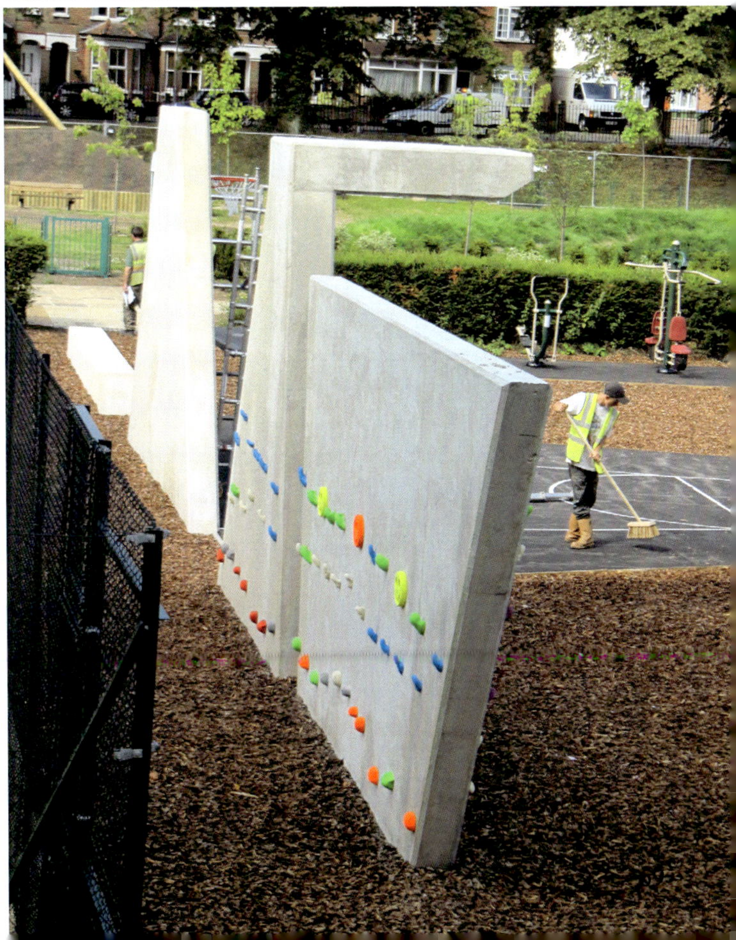

St James' Park – A Real 'Park for People' Project

Jon Dyer-Slade, Head of Neighbourhood Services, Southampton City Council, 2011

I was reflecting back on St James' Park (SJP) – which really is a fabulous 'Park for People' project. Over the six years of working with the Friends, there are certainly a lot of people who deserve a mention.

Before I do, I would also like to mention one person who wasn't a FoSJP member but was a true 'Friend' of the Park who is sadly no longer with us but who was instrumental in the concept of this project – Mike Spickett. Mike was our Landscape and Development Officer in the late 1990s and early Noughties and it must have been some time around the summer of 2002 that we met on site and he convinced me that SJP would be the best park to improve next – he had just finished the lottery funded refurbishment of Central Parks.

Mike sadly died in 2004 of cancer but he would have loved this park – it's fun, a bit edgy, quirky in places, innovative and has something for everyone with loads of opportunities for local people to get involved in keeping it a really great park for the local and wider community. Mike was also very keen to establish a friends group but I don't think even he recognised the massive potential within the St James' Park users for building such a strong friends group. There are many many local people who deserve a big thank you for helping make this such a success. But I'd better mention a few…

- I'd like to start with all the junior FoSJP members, some of whom were little tiny people when we started this project but are not so junior any more! Children and parks are made for each other and they are often the catalyst for other people coming into the Park too as parents, grandparents, aunties, uncles bring them along to play. The great thing about SJP now is that there are a few more things for the grown-ups to do too. The time and enthusiasm added by the young people in the design stages and at the various events has made this project fit for the local community. So a big thank you to all the children and young people who have helped get us to this point and they have a key role in making sure the Park is respected and looked after going into the future.

- From the young to the… history! Michaela's fantastic heritage project has discovered lots of previously unknown facts about the Park, and no doubt enjoyed many a conversation about the train station myths and other not quite right ideas. (Apparently there will be more on the train story in one of the next heritage books.) She has built up a fantastic history group around the project and discovered some lovely stories relating to the Park. Finally, Michaela and the team - working with local young people - have produced some brilliant historical records and used the information to create some great pieces of art for the Park - well done Michaela and the history volunteers who have been working with her.

- Martin Gardner – the man in the Park! Martin has had a foot in both camps for his work with the Friends and with Southampton City Council. His meticulous note taking updates were certainly needed in progressing the renovation project. This has helped us out on several occasions! Thanks Martin.

- Mike Smith - the 'calm can do man' of FoSJP for having the vision for the café and for taking on the role as Managing Director of ParkLife – I'm looking forward to popping into ParkLife for refreshments without discussing business. Big thank you to Mike and the new ParkLife team.

- Rebecca Kinge - for her contributions to the early lottery applications and research so that the committee could progress their ideas around the sort of organisation they wanted to be and that links into to all the other FoSJP Committee members over the many years who have spent hours and hours and hours sorting out the vision and direction for the Park, working out what the bite size steps to take were and then looking endlessly at plans and designs and giving their feedback - thank you all so much for all your volunteered time.

Then there are the members of the Friends who have helped with all the various events from the 'Putting the Park to Bed' event to the massive 'Park100 Green Space' celebration plus all the other community engagement things - well done to all of you.

The risk with these 'thank you's' is that you miss someone: well apologies if I have and thank you. But, I wanted to finish with a true 'Friend of the Friends' - Nichola Caveney. Nichola has been the driving force of the friends group and has maintained enthusiasm and commitment to the Park for all these years. There is so much we could say about Nichola's contribution but actually everyone knows how much effort and time she and her family have dedicated to this project – it is awesome! Nichola has also been incredibly hospitable in hosting many of the project meetings in her home and no one really wanted to offer an alternative because of the great soup she served up after many a cold HLF visit. Nichola's work is not yet done as there is the getting used to the Park, applying for the Green Flag and exploring the potential for the Friends to be actively engaged in the future maintenance and management of the Park.

7 A Long Standing Tradition of Carnivals and Community Events

Shirley Carnival

The Shirley Carnival was a community event designed to bring the whole community together. It involved local businesses and organisations decorating their vehicles which then entered in a colourful parade which travelled around Church Street and the Shirley High Street area until it reached its final destination of 'Shirley Rec'. As well as providing entertainment, a primary aim was to raise money for local charities. The Shirley Children's Hospital, later Southampton Children's Hospital, was regularly one of the main beneficiaries. The hospital also held its own charity fundraiser 'flag days' which have been described as being like a very 'smart' garden fête.

Shirley Carnival, c.1930 Photograph donated by Mrs Irene (Rene) Johnson. Mrs Johnson is pictured with her grandmother and her siblings after they won a prize for their miniature car in the Shirley Carnival, c.1930. Reproduced courtesy of the Southern Daily Echo

Peter Ross: *"Whilst looking through some old family photos recently I found a picture taken around about 1930 of my father's sister Elsie Ross. She appears to be standing in the Rec with the tennis courts and St James' Road behind her. I think she must have been attending some sort of function there as her clothes look rather unusual! Elsie was born in 1919 and unfortunately passed away due to illness, possibly meningitis, at the age of 13 so I would guess the photo would have been taken about 1929 - 32. Elsie & family lived at No.104 Warren Avenue, which they moved into as a new house around about 1927/8."*

At the FoSJP First Birthday Party event in May 2007, Mrs Hazel Crates kindly brought along some family photographs estimated to be taken in 1930. These feature her grandfather's dairy delivery truck participating in the Shirley Carnival and pictured in the Park and on procession in surrounding roads.

Shirley Carnival, c.1930
Left to right: Tom Hicks (Mrs Crates's father) and Dorothy Hicks (Mrs Crates's mother), in front of the Hicks Dairy Shirley Carnival Float 1930. Thought to be on Church Street, Shirley

Shirley Carnival, c.1930. Hicks Dairy's delivery truck from the Shirley Carnival, at the Park. Left - Tom Hicks (Mrs Crates's father). Second from right Mrs Dorothy Hicks (Mrs Crates's mother). Reproduced with kind permission of Mrs Hazel Crates (née Hicks) and the Southern Daily Echo

"A special memory was when my Grandfather's Dairy Float won first prize in the Shirley Carnival. After parading in the streets of Shirley, the carnival would finish in St James' Park, known then as Shirley Rec."

Shirley Carnival, c.1930 Left to right: Tom Hicks (Mrs Crates's father), Fred Hicks (Mrs Crates's uncle), Hazel about six years old in fancy dress, an unknown lady, Mrs Dorothy Hicks (Mrs Crates's mother), an unknown lady, and Aunt Beatrice (Fred Hicks's Wife)

When FoSJP began running larger community events in the Park in 2007, Mrs Hazel Crates came to visit FoSJP to thank us. She was emotional and very excited. The event had so reminded her of her childhood - she was thrilled to see the Park alive with people again. She returned with several extra photographs to share with us, including photographs of her as a child at Shirley School. Whenever FoSJP ran a community event, Mrs Crates would join us for a cup of tea: she couldn't thank FoSJP enough for the lovely days out and a reminder of those happy times of more than 70 years ago. In recent years Hazel became unwell and although she lived opposite the Park, she couldn't manage to get out. We haven't seen Hazel for some time now. We miss her joyfulness and appreciate all the photographs and memories shared with us.

Hazel Crates née Hicks

Hazel Crates

Shirley Military Band 1912. Courtesy of Southampton City Council Arts & Heritage

According to Mr Leonard's chapter, the first record of a request for a social event in the Park was from the 'Southampton Town Band playing there on a Wednesday evening, 8th August 1909.' One wonders if this Shirley Military Band also had an opportunity to play in the Park? Bands providing free outdoor performances were a popular entertainment in the Edwardian period. There's something quite magical about taking a fold-up chair or a picnic rug on a Sunday afternoon, or on a warm summer's evening, and listening to a concert in the Park. Interestingly, the original designs for the laying out of the Park in 1911 did include a bandstand, but this was not erected. FoSJP, SCC and the designers decided to rectify this and included two potential performance areas in the newly renovated Park: the café terrace and the gazebo at the northern end of the Botanical Walk.

FoSJP were thrilled when on 14th August 2011, just after the re-opening of the new Park, the Salisbury Band were able to provide a performance on the new café terrace. This event was well received and FoSJP members Brenda Bennett and Julie Catling suggested that FoSJP try and provide more of this type of event in the Park. There have since been several musical performances; bands and choirs have shared both the café terrace and the gazebo stage.

Other organisations that have run regular community events in the Park are the local churches and the Scouts. It would seem that this is not a recent occurrence. Another early social event was in 1913 when permission was granted for the Shirley Church Parade to take place there on 20 July, on behalf of local charities. Norman Burnett, former Park Keeper, remembers one church holding regular events during the summers in the 1990s. They essentially provided a holiday club for children. There has certainly been a need for summer play events. Prior to the renovations 'Jamies Playtime' organised by FoSJP's Rebecca Kinge and Surestart provided an excellent opportunity for little ones to get creative and for parents to socialise during school holidays. In recent years, the Shirley Churches Together organisation has also provided social events in the Park, with activities for children, teas, cakes and other refreshments.

For many years prior to the 2010-2011 renovations the Scouts were holding their annual summer fête in St James' Park. Bill Smith, born 1936, remembers using the Rec when he was in the 2nd Southampton Cubs. The headquarters were on Vaudrey Street and the Pack was led by Mr Dawkins, who is pictured at the rear (centre) of the photograph. This picture provided by Bill is estimated to be from 1943/44 and was taken in the Park on the old Winchester Road steps. Bill is on the far right of the back row of boys. Since the renovations the Scouts have helped run events in the Park for the local community.

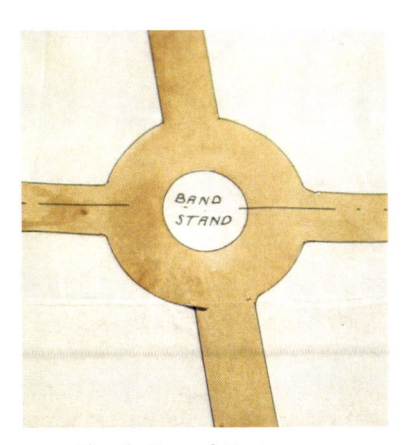

1911 Plans by Borough Engineer J A Crowther. SCC Archives

2nd Southampton Cubs on the old Winchester Road steps c.1943/44 (Courtesy of Bill Smith)

Since 2006, FoSJP have run many events in the Park, initially under the guidance of Nichola Caveney, the first Chair of FoSJP, and more recently via Marina Murphy, as a paid Community Volunteer Coordinator. Certainly in the beginning an army of volunteers would be recruited to make sure the day ran smoothly. The combination of tea, cake, stalls and activities for the children transformed the Park into what invariably felt like a village fête. These were festivities for all the community to venture out: really sociable and relaxed occasions. Always with something for everyone, these events were very popular with all age groups.

Some of the events stand out and are worthy of a mention. In May 2007, the first birthday event of FoSJP was a celebration of FoSJP's establishment and its achievements to date. Photographs appeared in the local newspaper and as on many of these occasions, Richard Hallett the baker who had been based on St James' Road, baked a celebration cake especially for the occasion. Cakes seemed to be a speciality at FoSJP events: Richard wasn't the only one baking in Shirley for them. A whole team of community bakers did everyone proud over and over again at many FoSJP events that were to follow. The refreshment tent, erected by Mike Smith and his team and beautifully decorated by Trudie Smith, Victoria Horne, Sophie Carrington, Helen Hazelwood, Esther Clift, and a whole team of supporting assistants was always one of the most popular stalls. When the Park was closed for renovations, the FoSJP team even took their teas and cakes, plus a barbecue and history display along to the former Civil Service Sports Ground - to spread the cheer further afield. (There is a pun in there.)

Green Nose Day

In 2009, the Green Nose Day event was a first for FoSJP in that it was the idea of a group of young people. Nichola Caveney was there to offer guidance every step of the way, to enable the organisers to take their ideas and turn them into reality. They did a fantastic job. It was a fun event with an 'environmental' theme: an event that everyone who took part in should be really proud of. They even recorded some pledges to help improve the environment - which can be viewed on the FoSJP website.

Park100

The July 2007 Park100 Event has been featured throughout this book and was probably the most significant event of FoSJP's early days. The replica Spitfire in the Park has been a memorable image for children and adults alike.

The Big Lunch

The Big Lunch 2009 event also marked a first. This was the first time that FoSJP was approached by members of the public and asked to support them in running an event in the Park. Residents of Church Street and Twyford Avenue were eager to participate in this national event. The Big Lunch centres around communities sharing food together, often outside, at a street party or a community picnic. One of those resident organisers, James Batchelor, later became one of the volunteer ParkLife Directors mentioned by Nichola Caveney.

Diwali Week

From 13-17th November 2012, the Park hosted Diwali events. The festival on the Saturday was a celebration of light; it brought music, dance, art and an array of vibrant colours to the Park.

New Park Communities

The renovation of St James' Park coincided with the arrival in Southampton of new communities from Eastern Europe. When consulted about the proposed 2010-2011 changes to the Park, those who completed questionnaires were very positive about the Park; local Polish shop owners enthusiastically reported that the Park was a popular venue for families and the field was regularly used by the young men for a Sunday game of football. In 2013, Community Coordinator Jan Carr keen to celebrate these new communities, at the Park, organised an Eastern European Photographers Exhibition, in partnership with Pavel Baran and Dave Adcock from EU Welcome. The event was officially opened by the Mayor of Southampton at a special preview evening and featured some very talented photographers and film makers. On Saturday 31st August, there was face painting for children and on Sunday the 1st September, local Polish band Ez Way performed under the Gazebo. Throughout the exhibition the ParkLife Café's menu had a European flavour. It is hoped that more of these artistic and cultural events will take place in the future.

On the theme of events, Tania Emery, Chair of FoSJP comments on how the need for events has changed:

"From the very beginning the Friends group has run events and organised activities with the aim of enhancing the enjoyment of the Park and to provide Park users with new opportunities. The re-development of the facilities in St James' Park have made it a destination park with people travelling from all over the city of Southampton and beyond: to visit the playground and free-to-use sports facilities and to enjoy the ParkLife café and community room. This means that the Park attracts a large number of visitors and the need to provide one-off events to encourage people to use the Park has reduced. However the Friends of St James' Park remains a vital and vibrant part of the life of the Park.

The Friends group has become the catalyst and link for many other community groups and individuals wishing to use the facilities that the Park can offer, thus providing new opportunities for a wider number of people. The Friends, in partnership with others, have been able to access funding to enable a range of activities to occur within the Park: these include working with children and young people with the Coxford and District Youth Project and Autism Hampshire; sporting opportunities through partnerships with the Lawn Tennis Association and others; and a wide range of other learning and support opportunities such as legal advice, job clubs and life skills learning. Much of this has been carried out as a result of a substantial grant from the Lankelly Chase Foundation which has allowed for the employment of a part-time Community Coordinator for a three-year period. In addition, FoSJP are developing a number of regular groups who work within the Park such as the Gardening Team who volunteer regularly to enhance the physical planted environment of the Park and those that volunteer at a monthly free-to-access craft group run on Saturday mornings. The Friends group also provides support to the café and community room Community Interest Company, ParkLife.

We are excited to see how St James' Park continues to support the community it serves and pleased to know that the Friends of St James' Park plays a key part in its continued success. The future for the Park is exciting with new opportunities to use the facilities and serve the community presenting themselves all the time. We are encouraged that new members continue to join the Friends, enthused by the work it is doing and bringing new skills and ideas with them."

"We hope that the Friends group will be around for a long time to come to continue to work to enhance the life of the Park for all who use it."

Rachel Smart and Dom Bowen pictured at the Noise Event 2007

8 Never Too Old to Learn - Education in the Park

St James' Park is the perfect space for outdoor education: there is a flat green field for team sports; numerous trees, plants and insects for nature studies; a community room for an indoor classroom and a café for refreshments. It has been used for sports, music, environmental education, art, history, orienteering, drama plays and dance. The Park has frequently inspired creativity and art. There is a long-standing history of the Park being used by local schools; a tradition that has continued. More recently, since the renovations provided a community room and café, it has also been used by a group of home schooled children and for various adult education workshops.

St James' Park And St Faith's School, Winchester Road

"In the early 1950s I went to a school called St Faith's which was opposite the Park in Wordsworth Road. The corner with Winchester Road. We used the Park for breaks, P.E. and school yearly games. Mr May was the teacher and he taught us rounders, physical exercise etc. In our break times we would run along the banks around the Park; there were two levels of banks well worn with use. Today these sides are at a slope no longer the banks I used as a child. My auntie lived in Didcot Road and I would go there after school and in summer holidays and we would often have picnics in the Park."
Marion Couper

Wordsworth Primary School

"I do not remember Wordsworth School children using St James' Park as we had wonderful school grounds, but I am sure Shirley First and Shirley Junior would have used it at some time, even though they sometimes used Wordsworth School grounds. Some members of Wordsworth staff used it for a half hour of tranquillity during the lunch hour on occasions."
Rita Judd

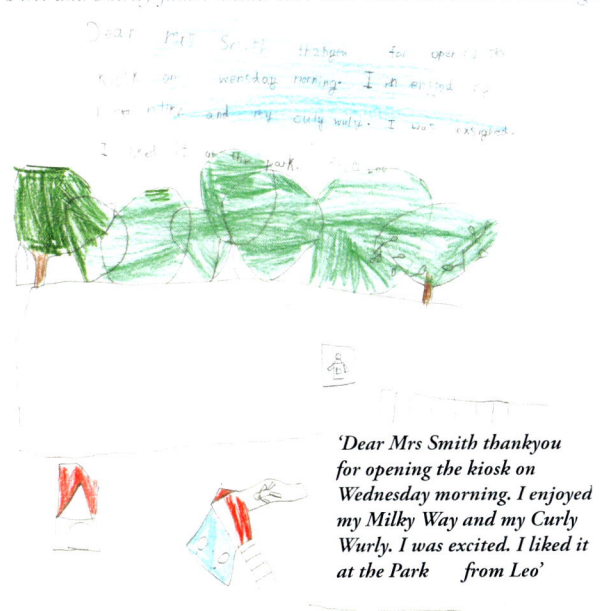

[Mrs Judd was Matron of Wordsworth First School around 1972, under the headship of Miss Joyce Percival. Mrs Judd succeeded the first matron of eighteen months, whose primary role was school nurse with clerical duties. In those days, Southampton didn't employ school secretaries in First Schools, only matrons. However, things moved on and Mrs Judd's role became secretarial with responsibility for children's welfare. In 1972, there were 365 children on the school roll.]

In recent years children from Wordsworth School (Infant - now Primary) have been regular visitors to St James' Park, often under the instruction of Mrs Trudie Smith. Mrs Smith was one of the original founding FoSJP Committee members and an enthusiastic 'Friend' of the Park. Mrs Smith was very keen for her students to have a real appreciation of their Park and to understand what plants need to grow well. When the FoSJP kiosk first opened in 2006, Mrs Smith arranged educational trips for the Infant children, aged 4-7, including a visit to the Park Kiosk to practise handling money. They used the Kiosk as a training ground to buy an ice lolly, giving money and receiving and checking change. One of the most important things was to practise saying 'please' and 'thank-you' when making their purchases (they were great at it). After the trip, some of the children wrote thank-you letters to Mrs Smith, which were posted on the wall inside the Kiosk. When the Kiosk was taken down in 2010 these were rescued from the wall.

'Dear Mrs Smith thankyou for opening the kiosk on Wednesday morning. I enjoyed my Milky Way and my Curly Wurly. I was excited. I liked it at the Park   from Leo'

'To Mrs Smith I enjoyed my icecream You really work hard from Chloe'

Fond Memories of Shirley Recreation Ground (St James' Park) in the 1950s

"I have many fond memories of the Park since a child in the 1950s, when I attended Shirley Junior School. During the summer term we were marched down to the Park to play rounders. Does anyone remember a Miss Bidwell who lived at the corner of Bellemoor Road? She used to invite the local Sunday School children around for a party in her gardens. The summer fêtes held at the vicarage in Church Street? The sweet shop on the corner where [Shirley] Parish Office is now? Playing tennis on one of the grass courts? I well remember the 'Gents' loo which was in a French style made of black wrought iron, at the corner of St James' Road and Winchester Road, and often used by the Sunday afternoon football players! The children's area of the Park declined in the late 1960s, but went through a revamp in the 1970s, and my children spent many happy hours there when visiting their grandparents. I'm delighted that St James' Park is safe and is going to have a well-deserved facelift. It is such an asset for the people of Shirley."
Jean Scott (née Brown), 2010

[Editor's Note - Jean now lives in Beverley, East Yorkshire; she caught up with St James' Park via our website.]

Picnic, play and games in the Park - Shirley Infant School - c.early 1990s

Leading up to the Park renovations, a total of 480 year 3 pupils from Shirley Junior School (aged 7-8) came to the Park for outdoor history lessons in 2007, 2008, 2009 and 2010. At this time, both Wordsworth and Shirley Infant Schools were feeder schools for Shirley Juniors. In the final lesson in 2010, the children also learnt about what the new Park was going to look like.

The children sent these beautiful thankyou cards.

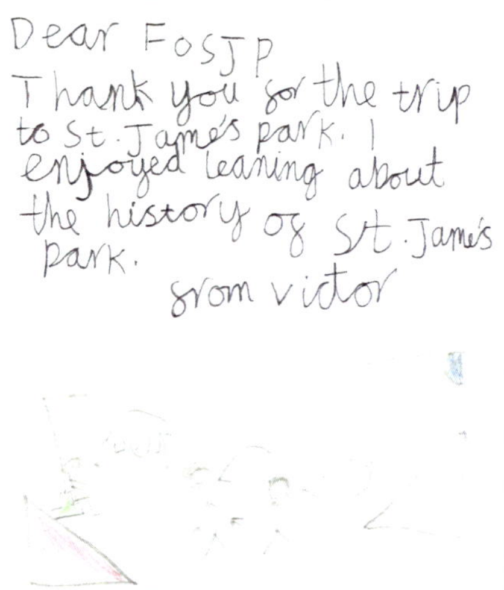

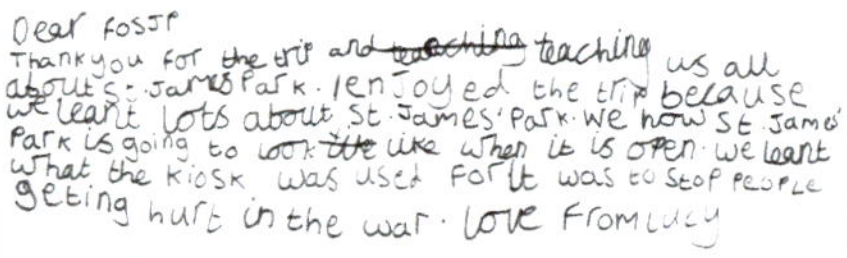

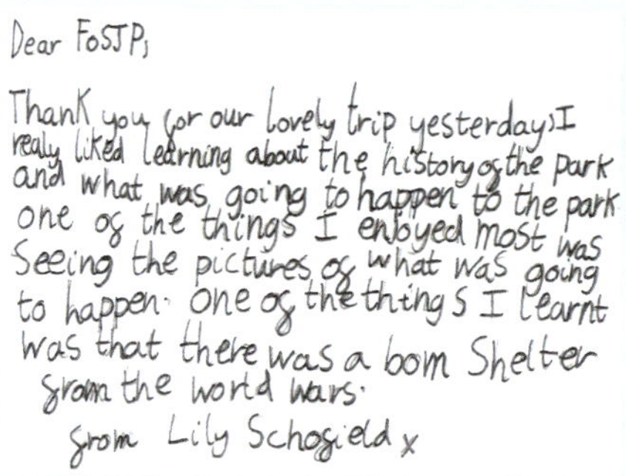

Upper Shirley Learning Community Christmas Event & Trust Launch

In December 2011, several of the local schools joined together to form an educational trust. On Friday 2nd December 2011, St James' Park hosted the Upper Shirley Learning Community's Christmas event and launch of the USLC Trust - since named the Jefferys Educational Trust (after Nathaniel and Catherine Jefferys). At this event there were musical performances - choirs and orchestra - from each of the USLC schools and Taunton College's community band; entertainment was provided by a juggler, a princess, and a suspiciously large reindeer; fairy lights lit up the Park; and free hot food, courtesy of the Trust's sponsors, was served from the ParkLife Café.

Of course many children from these schools and others have partaken in informal educational activities at FoSJP events, be that an orienteering course, a leaf trail, park quiz, or crafts in the Park - usually designed by the professional hands of FoSJP Members (and teachers) Jill Gardner or Nichola Caveney. The tradition of crafts started with the very young at events like Jamie's Playtime. This was a holiday play-scheme for toddlers with a 'messy play' focus and organised by FoSJP volunteer Rebecca Kinge in partnership with Surestart. Monthly 'Crafty Saturday' sessions have also been held at the Park.

Upper Shirley Learning Community's Christmas event December 2011

Tudor Costume Workshop September 2012

In September 2012, Dr Mary South ran a Tudor Costume Workshop in the ParkLife Community Room. With help from textile design expert Jason Butler from the University of Southampton, old clothes and material scraps were re-created into Tudor-style costumes. Attendees were then invited to take part in a Tudor procession at the Michaelmas Fair in Southampton. Ladies of the 'Make Do and Mend' class helped with the sewing.

Tudor Costume Workshop participants display their costumes and accessories at the Michaelmas "Procession of St.Ledger"

Procession photographs by Cheryl Butler

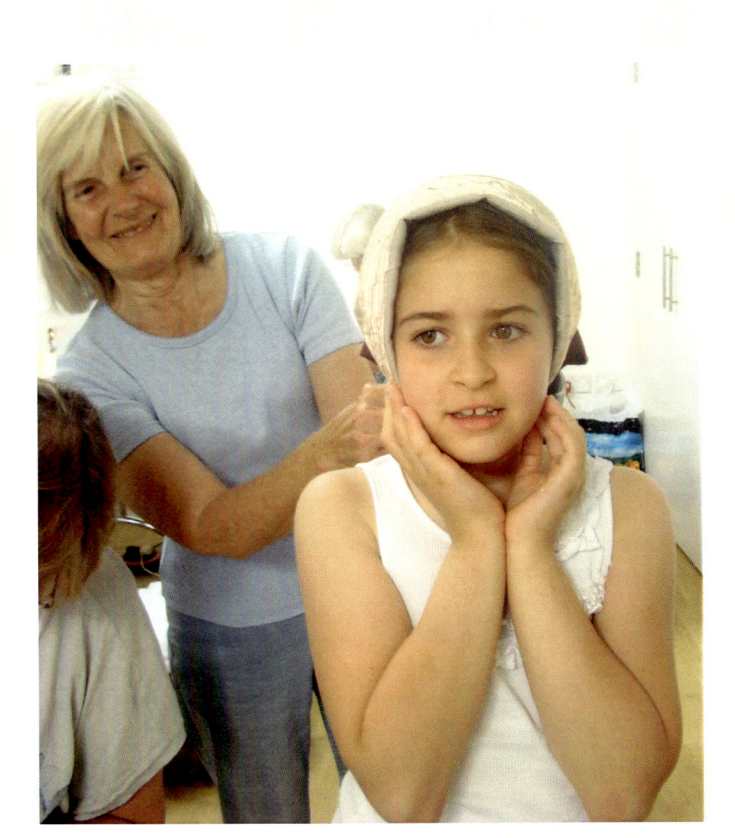

Learn to Love Learning

Learn to Love Learning Craft Workshop

Don Smith shares Southampton stories at the Learn to Love Learning Workshops, ParkLife Café and Community Room, St James' Park (2013)

Art for the Park - The Café Windows
Sarah Silverstein Designs

These creative designs installed on the windows of the ParkLife Café, St James' Park in 2011, are by Sarah Silverstein then an illustration student from Southampton Solent University. FoSJP particularly wanted to give a young artist or illustrator the opportunity to work on a high profile piece of public art and Sarah was chosen by her tutors as a student with talent, potential and motivation. Sarah worked with the Friends of St James' Park, under the guidance of her supervisors, Peter Lloyd and Jonny Hannah. Sarah donated her artwork and her time freely to the project.

The design challenge for the building had been "to deliver something of great value to the community yet retain the integrity of our heritage," (Design Engine Architects Ltd). The designs of the new additions to the building reflected this heritage: the café terrace roof is shaped like an aeroplane wing; the rails of the café terrace resemble those found on a ship or liner; the skylights that bring natural light into the former bomb shelter are reminders of the searchlights that once sought out enemy planes in dark Southampton skies. The brief for Sarah was to also reflect this period of the building's history. The artworks that Sarah developed show the links between the Park building and its Second World War origins as an Air Raid Precautions (ARP) building. During this period the RAF/WAAF also operated a barrage balloon in the Park to deter enemy planes.

The first 'post - renovation' history lesson in St James' Park

2013 Back to the Classroom for L-R Don Smith, aged 85; Ken Conway, aged 90; and Arthur House, aged 93

In May 2013, more than 20 children and their parents found out about the Park and its links to the past by listening to older people's stories. Many questions were asked of our guests: Don talked about his painting of what 'Shirley Rec' was like in 1934; Ken shared more about the Second World War origins of the building as an ARP Report and Control Centre, and his own experience of a similar post in the Foundry Lane area; Arthur shared his personal story of a special bench in the Park and how the students of Upper Shirley High School replaced it. Arthur also brought along a reporter from BBC Radio Solent, who was interviewing him about his football days playing for Southampton FC. The reporter also interviewed some of the children asking Arthur questions. After telling his story to all the children, Arthur had to rush off for his own interview!

"My greatest passion has always been drawing, and I am particularly interested in reportage illustration: drawing people and places through direct observation. For this project for St James' Park, I took the opportunity to explore Southampton and Shirley (an area fairly new to me), and draw buildings and monuments on site with pen, ink and wash. Although the process of drawing, re-drawing, editing and putting together the final image was something that took months to finish, I have thoroughly enjoyed the whole process. To see my drawings on such a grand scale makes me proud to know my hard work has been for a good cause! I am honoured to have been given this opportunity of working on this live brief for St James' Park in Shirley, and to have been able to apply something I love doing to such a great project (where younger and older generations were able to work together in remembering and recreating the past). What was so great about this project is that I could get really involved by researching the local history of Southampton and meeting people involved in the War, who had memories to share with me which could be incorporated into my artwork." Sarah Silverstein 2011

More of Sarah's art can be viewed on her website at www.beginwithadot.com

Southampton SOLENT University

Art for the Park
The Upper Shirley High School Project

Ken Conway and Arthur House were invited to share their stories with a group of students from Upper Shirley High School during the 'Art for the Park' project. The aim of this project was to produce a piece of art for the zipwire wall that would reflect both the history of the Park and local people's stories of how the Park has been used over time. Artist Anna Vickers was employed to work with members of the FoSJP History Team and with the students to interpret the Park's history.

Ken Conway   *Arthur House*

Students worked with FoSJP at Upper Shirley High School and learnt how to ask open ended questions during an oral history interview. Ken and Arthur came along to the session as the interviewees.

Ken and Arthur shared their memories of St. James' Park from the 1930s and 1940s with the students and the students had a chance to ask them questions.

Students used their own experience and the stories, as discussed by Ken and Arthur, to create silhouettes - using photography which depicted some of the activities which have taken place in the Park throughout time.

Students were asked what they would like to see included in the artwork and were shown the location in which it would be placed. Parents talking, people exercising and dog walking were initial ideas that the students wanted to include.

Other ideas included:

Representations of the local native SO15 flora and fauna.

Cherry trees, roses and daffodils which have been admired in the Park by many generations.

A park bench (this comes from Arthur's interview with the young people and the significance it holds in his life story).

A cow and calf representing when the Park was once a pasture.

Both students and Park users suggested adding plants to the area in front of the zipwire wall.

Elements of the Design

The general structure of the design is inspired by ironwork designs from the Victorian and Edwardian periods and the Art Deco style. Interwoven into the design are silhouettes that reflect stories told by older people about how the Park has been used over time. The land was purchased for the purpose of a Recreation Ground in 1907, during the Edwardian period. However, it was in 1911 that its preparation for public use was complete. In 2011, a century later, the Park was restored and enhanced. The final artwork was made from water-jet cut metal (aluminium), which was black powder coated.

Working on the Art for the Park project provided fantastic opportunities for older and younger generations to meet, talk and to get to know each other better. It forged greater understanding of each others' lives. The students were amazed by the jobs that both Ken and Arthur had done during the Second World War: working long shifts, followed by being on watch all night; experiencing being bombed out of a house; witnessing bombing; or putting out fires with a bucket of sand. They couldn't imagine living in the way that Ken and Arthur had done. But the learning wasn't one way. One of the things that our older people said was how sorry they felt for the younger generations - who had to learn so much these days at school! Arthur found these children to be the politest group of teenage children he had ever met and Ken was impressed at how much school dinners had improved! Working on this project was to have much bigger implications than any of us could have imagined. In order to find out more we need to share Arthur's story to understand the full value of the educational projects in the Park.

Arthur, Ken and the chaps didn't stop there - they even went to University

Well actually the history students of the University of Southampton came to them, at the Shirley Parish Hall, to find out about their memories of VE Day. The bunting in these photographs was made especially for the event by Hilary Moore and her group of 'Make Do and Mend' ladies.

9   Arthur's Bench - A Park Love Story

Arthur House - Interviewed in June 2009 (aged 89) by Michaela A Lawler-Levene and in February 2011 (aged 91) by the students of Upper Shirley High School

"I was born in March 1920. My Dad's name was Harry James House and my mother's name was Ellen Amelia Harris. I lived in Southampton… at Foundry Lane to start with and then Freemantle. When I was younger there didn't seem as many people… nobody seemed to have cars. I was five before I had my first ride in a car. My grandson had flown across the Atlantic four times before he was five. We had to walk everywhere. There was a lot of clean fun.

I loved football. I played for my school, Freemantle School, I played for Portswood Juvenile club. I played for Lymington Town, and I got picked up by a scout and became professional in 1938. I was the goalkeeper for Southampton. I played on right up until I went into the Navy and occasionally during the Navy times."

USH: Can you tell me where you used to play?

"There was a field opposite when I lived in Fairfield Square, and it eventually became the big cigarette factory [British American Tobacco]. Before it was built we used to go there and play (where we shouldn't have done). We went to Freemantle and often we would go down and play on the mud flats."

USH: Do you have a favourite memory?

"Favourite memory? Of my playing days? Or of my life?"

USH: When you were a child.

"My favourite memory was meeting my girlfriend."

USH: Could you tell me how you met your girlfriend and what it was like?

"How did I meet her? I was walking along and I saw this pretty girl going by on her bike and I did what you chaps do, gave her the wolf-whistle and eventually made a date. My life has actually gone around in a circle. I was born in Southampton, I met my future wife here in Southampton.

'Actually, my first date was in St James' Park'

In 1935, I made a date with this young girl, about 15 years of age, and established she lived over the far side of Ice House Hill and I lived in Victor Street, this side, so we met on the top of Ice House Hill and she came along with her four siblings and I thought to myself, 'What have I let myself in for?' So we walked up to… the Park, the Recreation Ground as we knew it then, and we sat on the seat just inside, on the Winchester Road end. We walked up Winchester Road and just in that entrance there. The two younger ones were still in the pram: one asleep, the other two were playing ball - and that was our first date on the first seat inside of St James' Park.

We got married in 1940 at St James' Church and moved to Northumberland Road.

We moved to Northumberland Road on August 10th and late October the Germans blew that house up. A week later I was in the Navy, the Royal Navy, Fleet Air Arm. My job was on the flight deck, repairing planes before they went out off the flight deck and repairing them when they came back.

After the War I was working as Area Manager for Whitbread's, the big brewery company. I had my own pub for 18 years. I emigrated to Canada when I retired. My only son Terry emigrated to Canada and we followed him out there, to Vancouver Island, for 27 years. He passed away in January 2006 and my wife passed away in December 2006, which left me there with no family. So I came back and brought her ashes back to the church here. She always wanted to go back to the church we were married in and the Vicar very kindly let me go in there. My nephew Robert and his younger daughter Helen came in there with me, then I took her ashes up to my parents grave, which is up at Hollybrook. That's how I got very close to Robert and family again, I rekindled with them and Jenny, his sister and I've got a large family now. I've got great-grand nieces and all that.

I was born and bred in Southampton, I played football for Southampton; my whole life has centred round Southampton. I'm now living right near where I was as a teenager. As a teenager I lived in Victor Street, where the surgery is now and that's where I took my first girlfriend, Winnie, to meet my parents for

Arthur and Winnie get married at St James' Church 1940

Arthur shares his memories with students from Upper Shirley High School

When Arthur shared this story with the students and staff of Upper Shirley High School, it made a lasting impression on them. They were very moved by Arthur's humanity and the love he had for his wife. Arthur had very carefully unwrapped a letter that he had sent to his wife when he had been in the Navy. He had drawn a picture of a church on it, to remind her of when they had got married. Winnie had kept the letter all her life and when she died Arthur found it amongst her belongings. Arthur carefully unwrapped some delicate and fragile personal mementos that he has carried in his wallet since World War Two: his son's first baby shoe, the beautiful letter that he had written to his wife whilst at war, and the last '10 bob note' that his father had given him on one of his 'home on leave' visits - all items of personal significance.

the first time, where the surgery is. So I've come right the way round in a circle and that's how I got connected to the Park - that one seat was our favourite seat. I always tease people, I tease Robert and Jill as we went by. I used to say:

'See that seat there, that's where Winnie and I had our first date'

and now that's fallen to pieces and that's why I was interested if I could put towards a new seat and put a plaque in memory of her there.

Since I've lived in Milner Court, every nice afternoon, that's where I've always walked, up round the Park and sat on my favourite seat for half an hour for a rest then walked back home again. It was coming from there that one day when I found the seat had gone and I bumped into the Vicar, who also knew me as Uncle Arthur, and he said 'Hello Uncle Arthur' and I told him the story about the seat and it was him that brought me in touch with your meeting over there."

[Editor's note – the meeting that Arthur refers to was a history exhibition on May 16th 2009 at the Shirley Parish Hall.]

Arthur and Winnie with their young son Terry

These sentiments really touched the students and staff. They were really concerned that Arthur's bench was no longer there for him to sit on and remember Winnie, who had clearly meant so much to him. After the visit to the school, the children asked their teachers if they could help Arthur raise some money for a new bench in the Park. They organised a 'non-school uniform' day and when they had raised the money they invited Arthur back to the school for a 'school lunch' and a surprise presentation.

Arthur's bench reinstated in the Park with a plaque for his wife, Winnie House née Payne

89

Arthur went on to share his and Winnie's story with a group of students from the University of Southampton, to a group of adults at the Learn to Love Learning Group at St James' Park and with a group of home schooled children and their parents, also at St James' Park. Arthur's recorded story was also taken to a conference at the University of Sunderland in 2011 to show the unexpected positive outcomes from sharing older people's stories. Arthur and the children had mutual respect and the children of Upper Shirley High School showed everyone how great some of our youngsters today can be. When the Park was re-opened in 2011 after major renovations, Arthur was one of two interviewees invited, with two children from Upper Shirley High School and younger children who had won a competition, to cut the ribbon that officially re-opened the Park. Then Arthur took all that information, photographs of working with the children, his story in print back to Vancouver Island, to show the ladies who had cared for his wife. The good news from St James' Park, Shirley, spreads around the globe!

Arthur at the opeining ceremony of the Park in 2011

But that's not the end of the story...

On Saturday 25th October 2014, Arthur sent us this account via his nephew, Bob Grice.

Arthur House - An Encounter in St James' Park

"I was sitting on my bench in the Park this morning enjoying the mild weather and sunshine. A lady on an invalid scooter pulled up and said hello. I took pleasure in telling her the story of my bench.

She told me that her frail old dog which had been slowly padding beside the buggy was the equivalent of 91 in human years.

I said that I was 94 and she replied that she was 92. We got on really well and the subject of our years in this part of Southampton was discussed. I told her that until I was 20 and conscripted into the Navy I had lived in number 40 Winchester Road.

This was met with shock for she revealed that she lived at that address for many years after buying the house in 1948 for £1,000.

We both remembered the layout of the rooms especially a small room at the back of the house which had been mine. I was a painter and decorator in those days and she described exactly how my decorating efforts were still there in 1948.

We chatted non-stop for over an hour and found we had many more things in common. For example, we were both married in St James' Parish Church. Me in 1940 and her in 1945.

I didn't catch the lady's name but I'm sure our paths will cross again."

and so the stories from St James' Park continue...

Endnotes

Chapter 1

1. Karen Wardley, 'Shirley: archaeological evidence for human activity from prehistoric to late Saxon times (c.700,000BC to c.1000AD)' not yet published.
2. (Anon) *Shall He Find Faith? An Appeal from two Southampton Parishes* (Southern Newspapers Ltd, 1935).
3. J. Guilmant and H. Kavanah (eds), *Shirley from Domesday to D-Day* (Southampton City Council, 1997). Chapter by Rosaleen Wilkinson, entitled 'Hill and Upper Shirley', page 2.
4. The 1778 map reveals a series of what appears to be four ponds.
5. Adrian Rance, *Shirley 1836 – 1986 Parish Church of Shirley 150th Anniversary* (The Parochial Church Council of St. James Church, Shirley, Southampton, June 1986).
6. *Shirley from Domesday to D-Day*, pages 7-18.
7. Ibid.
8. Ibid.
9. Hollybrook House itself tells a fascinating history, which will be partially detailed in a future book.
10. *Shirley from Domesday to D-Day*, page 11.
11. *Hampshire Advertiser*, 8th August 1836.
12. Freda Hancock Collection. Freda's Great Grandfather, Charles Jurd, lived at the top of Warren Avenue and was a gardener in one of the houses on The Crescent, Shirley Warren.
13. *Shirley 1836-1986 Parish Church of St. James Shirley 150th Anniversary*, page 5.
14. As advised by Mrs J. Catling, of Bellemoor Road. The conservation area was established in 1988 after a local residents' campaign to save houses built c 1835, on Bellemoor Road. Southampton City Council have also produced a Conservation area appraisal dated 1996.
15. Research notes – Ray Hancock (FoSJP History Team).
16. See number 14.
17. *Parish of Millbrook Tithe Records*, 1840-43. Southampton City Council, City Archives.
18. Covenant of 1851, Southampton City Council records.
19. T.B. Sands, *The Didcot, Newbury and Southampton Railway* (Oakwood Press, 1971).
20. A.G.K. Leonard, *Shirley Nuisances and Services: Shirley Health and Local Government in Victorian Shirley* (Southampton City Council, undated) page 20.
21. Ibid.
22. *Shirley from Domesday to D-Day*, pages 23-28.
23. Ibid.
24. 'Shirley: archaeological evidence for human activity from prehistoric to late Saxon times (c.700,000BC to c.1000AD)'. Also, Southampton Heritage Environment Record - ref MSH138.
25. *Southampton Advertiser*, 14th April 1906.

Chapter 2

Footnote

Stratton Road was originally Station Road, the Borough Council having renamed it in 1903 because this had become obsolete and misleading. With Didcot and Newbury Roads, it is often thought to have been associated with the abortive plans of the Didcot, Newbury and Southampton Railway in the 1880s but in fact it predates this assumed connection by some thirty years. Shown as such on the 1867 Ordnance Survey map (reproduced at page 2 of the booklet *'Shirley Nuisances and Services'*), Station Road was originally named from the old police station fronting it near its junction with what was then Albert Street – renamed Victor Street in 1901. (Police) Station Road was one of the score of street on which the Shirley Local Board of Health erected painted slate name panels in 1859.

Chapter 3

1. *St James' Park Conservation Management Plan* 2008.
2. Leonard, A.G.K., Summer 2007, The Genesis of Shirley Recreation Ground in the *'Journal of the Southampton Local History Forum.'*
3. Peter Wardall collection.
4. Photo reproduced courtesy of Mrs Hazel Hayter, Shirley Infant and Junior Schools.
5. See endnote 2.

Chapter 4

1. The escaped Barrage Balloon was verified by a letter found in the Hampshire Archives, Winchester, by Geoff Gravelson, University of Southampton. The letter is a request from the Church of England requesting compensation for the damage.
2. Jake Simpkin Southampton during WW2 at http://www.bbc.co.uk/history/ww2peopleswar/
3. Ray Hancock research notes.
4. *Shirley from Domesday to D-Day* page 77.
5. Confirmed in the 1925 Kelly's Southampton Street Directory.

General note

The editors acknowledge that the spelling of 'St.' in St James' Park would normally be punctuated with a full stop to demonstrate the contraction of the word 'Saint'. The full stop has been omitted in this book to be consistent with the spelling of St James' Park on park welcome signs. Where St James' Park has been contracted to 'the Park' a capital letter 'P' has been used to demonstrate this specifically refers to St James' Park. The same principle has been used for the contraction of Shirley Recreation Ground to the 'Rec' or the 'Recreation Ground.'

Bibliography

Books

Anon., *Shall He Find Faith? An Appeal from two Southampton Parishes* (Southern Newspapers Ltd, 1935)

Barfield, Norman, *Supermarine* The Archive Photographs Series (Chalford Publishing, Trowbridge, 1996)

Brown, Jim, *Henry Brain A Victorian & Edwardian Photographer* (Bitterne Local History Society, Southampton, 2000)

Brown, Mike, *Put That Light Out! Britain's Civil Defence Services at War 1939-1945* (Sutton Publishing, Stroud, 1999)

Butler, Dr Cheryl, *"We only wore shoes on a Sunday" Oral Testimonies from Itchen Ferry, Southampton"* (The Diaper Heritage Association, Southampton, 2007)

Channer, Nick, *Francis Frith's Around Southampton* (Frith Book Co., Salisbury, 2000)

Dymond, David, *Researching and Writing History, A Practical Guide for Local Historians* (British Association for Local History, Salisbury, 1999)

Frankland, Claire, Hyslop, Donald and Jemima, Sheila *Southampton Blitz The Unofficial Story* (Oral History, Southampton City Council, Local Studies Section, Southampton 1990)

Gadd, Eric Wyeth, *Southampton – 100 years ago* (Southampton, 1978)

Guilmant, J. and Kavanah, H. (eds), *Shirley from Domesday to D-Day* (Southampton City Council, 1997)

Horne, John B., *100 Years of Southampton Transport* (City of Southampton 1979)

Howarth, Ken, *Oral History* (Sutton Publishing, Stroud, 1999)

Kemp, Anthony, *Southampton at War 1939-1945* (Ensign Publications, Southampton, 1989)

Leonard, A.G.K., *Southampton* (Images of England Series, Tempus Publishing, Stroud, 1997)

Leonard, A.G.K., *Southampton in old picture postcards* (European Library, Zaltbommel, Netherlands, 1992)

Leonard, A.G.K., *Stories of Southampton Streets* (Paul Cave Publications Ltd., Southampton, 1984)

Leonard, A.G.K., *Shirley Nuisances and Services: Shirley Health and Local Government in Victorian Shirley* (Southampton City Council, undated)

Peckham, Ingrid, *Southampton and D-Day* (Oral History, Southampton City Council, Southampton, 1994)

Platt, Colin, *Medieval Southampton, The port and trading community, AD 1000-1600* (Routledge and Kegan Paul, London and Boston, 1973)

Rance, A., *Shirley 1836 – 1986 Parish Church of Shirley 150th Anniversary* (The Parochial Church Council of St. James Church, Shirley, Southampton, June 1986)

Sandell, Elsie M., *Southampton Cavalcade* (Southampton, 1953)

Sandell, Elsie M., *Southampton Through the Ages* (Southampton, 1960)

Sands, T.B., *The Didcot, Newbury and Southampton Railway* (Oakwood Press, 1971)

Shrimpton, Jayne, *Family Photographs & How to Date Them* (Countryside Books, Newbury, 2008)

Stewart, Brian & Cutten, Mervyn, *The Shayer Family of Painters,* (F Lewis Publishers, London, 1981)

Vale, J., *The Country Houses of Southampton* (Proceedings of the Hampshire Field Club and Archaeological Society, Volume 39, 1983)

Vickers, John A., *The Religious Census of Hampshire 1851* (Hampshire County Council, Winchester, 1993)

White, Bill, Jemima, Sheila and Hyslop, Donald, *Dream Palaces, Going to the Pictures in Southampton'* (Oral History, Southampton City Council, Southampton, 1996)

Forthcoming Chapters in Books

Wardley, Karen 'Shirley: archaeological evidence for human activity from prehistoric to late Saxon times (c700,000BC to c 1000AD)' unpublished

Journal Articles

Leonard, A.G.K., 'The Genesis of Shirley Recreation Ground' in *the Journal of the Southampton Local History Forum* (Summer 2007)

Journal of the Oral History Society (various volumes).

Newspaper Articles

Hampshire Advertiser, 8th August 1836

'Death and Funeral of Mr George Harris' *Southampton Advertiser*, 14th April 1906

Websites

Friends of St James' Park website
http://www.fosjp.org.uk

Kelly's 1925 Southampton Street Directory **http://www.plimsoll.org/Southampton/streetdirectories/Directory1925/**

Simpkin, J. 'Southampton During WW2' **http://www.bbc.co.uk/history/ww2peopleswar/**

Southampton Heritage Environment Record - ref MSH138 Southampton City Council **http://www.southampton.gov.uk/planning/heritage/default.aspx**

Reports

St James' Park Conservation Management Plan 2008 Southampton City Council

Illustrations and Maps

Please see individual photographs, maps and endnotes for titles and sources.

Acknowledgements

This book was inspired by the enthusiasm of people attending the FoSJP history display at the Park100 centenary event in 2007, particularly Mr and Mrs Quick, Norman Burnett and Ken Conway. The display was produced thanks to the time and resources generously shared by Robert (Bob) Grice, Dr Mary South and Mrs Hazel Crates. As a then foundling history group, the first FoSJP History Subcommittee (Martin Caveney, Johnny Carrington, Dan Levene, Michaela A. Lawler-Levene) would like to acknowledge the advice given to FoSJP by local historians, especially Mr A.G.K. Leonard who has continued to support our project and Autumn Lecture Series. We also acknowledge the positive encouragement received from Jeff Pain and Jake Simpkin. For helping FoSJP realise the dream of recording local stories we acknowledge the training given by Padmini Broomfield of the Oral History Society. A huge thank you goes to the volunteer oral history typists especially: Kaye Barnett, Cindy Phillips, Jillianne Pickard and Vicki Stacey (the Oral History Typist Coordinator) and to Martin Gardner for his skill in presenting the historical information on the FoSJP website. To Nichola Caveney, Jon Dyer-Slade, Phil Heaton and Helen Saward gratitude for including the Shirley Heritage Project in the Parks for People Lottery Project and to Mike Harding, our advisor from the Heritage Lottery Fund, who totally shared our vision and enthusiasm for discovering these local photographs and stories. We acknowledge the work of those who have gone before us in uncovering Shirley's local history, especially John Guilmant, Adrian Rance, Elsie M. Sandell and Rosalind Wilkinson.

Production Team:

History Researchers and Editorial Team: Raymond Hancock, Madge Heath, Michaela A. Lawler-Levene, Dan Levene, Vicki Stacey, Peter Wardall. **Supported by:** Theresa Bowen, Lynda Chantler, Ken Conway, Martin Gardner, Helen Hazelwood, Erika Howells, Isidore C. Levene, Shiphra A. Levene, Margaret Osmond, Don Smith, Mary Smith, Bet Stacey, Liz Webb, Patricia White, Barrie Worth.
Photography: FoSJP official photographer - David Wheatley. **Additional photos from;** Cheryl Butler, Martin and Nicola Caveney, Patrick Douglas, Martin Gardner, Geoff Gravelson, Helen Hazelwood, Phil Heaton, Michaela A. Lawler-Levene, Cindy Phillips, Helen Saward, Trudie Smith, Anna Vickers, Andy Vowels, Peter Wardall, Lawrence Weedy.

Organisational Support:

Funders: Heritage Lottery Fund, Big Lottery Fund
Hampshire Archives and Local Studies: David Rymill
Hampshire Cultural Trust formally Winchester City Council: Robin Iles
Southampton City Council – current and former employees: Parks and Open Spaces Team; Norman Burnett, Stuart Davies, Ken Prior, Jon Dyer-Slade, Helen Saward; Karen Wardley Head of Collections; **City Archives:** Susan Hill, Joanne Smith; **Southampton City Art Gallery:** Tim Craven; **Southampton Central Library Local Studies Collection:** David Hollingworth; **Maritime and Local Collections:** Lindsay Ford, Maria Newberry; **Southampton Heritage Environment Record:** Ingrid Peckham
Shirley Infant and Junior School: Christine Bulmer, Hazel Hayter, Julie McKay and Gill Robinson
Shirley Parish Church: Theresa Bowen, Rev. Dan Clark and Rev. David Hazelwood (retired)
Southern Daily Echo: Keith Hamilton
Southampton Solent University: Peter Lloyd, Jonny Hannah and Sarah Silverstein
University of Southampton: Dr Jonathan Conlin, Dr Dan Levene, Dr Jane McDermid, Karen Robson, Jenny Ruthven, Prof Adrian Smith
Upper Shirley High: Art for the Park Project: Staff: Mariella De Ruiter, Lynn Brown and Mrs Clothier; **Students:** Matthew, David, Eliot, Rose, Shannon, Sian, Holly, Dan
Wild Plant Discovery: Celia Cox
Wordsworth Primary School: Paul Betteridge, Ruth Martin, Trudie Smith

Every effort has been made to ensure all contributors of articles and photographic images have been acknowledged. If we have inadvertently infringed anyone's copyright in respect of reproduction in these pages, compilers and publishers hope they will be excused.

Personal Contributors:

Audrey Behan
Norman Burnett
Sarah Cartwright
Ken Conway
Joan Cook
Vicki Cooper
Doreen Couper
Marion Couper
Hazel Crates
Nora Davies
Derek Doswell
Nigel Fayle
Martin Gardner

Jean Glue
Joan Greenings
Robert (Bob) Grice
Freda Hancock
Raymond Hancock
Wendy Hobbs
Arthur House
Judy Humby
Irene Johnson
Rita Judd
Gwendoline Kitchener
Mick Masters
Sarah Mintram

Hilary Moore
Marina Murphy
Jo Ormond
Cindy Phillips
Susan Ponsford
Ken Prior
Peter Ross
Jean Scott
Sarah Silverstein
Mary South
Donald (Don) R. Smith
William (Bill) Smith
Lesley Stapley

Anna Vickers
Gwendolyn Wardley
Peter Wardall
Janet Yendell
Robin Yendell